Grammar Rants

Grammar Rants

*How a Backstage Tour of Writing Complaints
Can Help Students Make Informed, Savvy
Choices About Their Writing*

Patricia A. Dunn and Ken Lindblom

Boynton/Cook Publishers
HEINEMANN
PORTSMOUTH, NH

Boynton/Cook Publishers, Inc.
361 Hanover Street
Portsmouth, NH 03801–3912
www.boyntoncook.com

Offices and agents throughout the world

© 2011 by Patricia A. Dunn and Ken Lindblom

The authors and publisher wish to thank those who have generously given permission to reprint borrowed material:

"Gramme(a)r: Using *Its* and *It's*" by Dan Bergan from the *Hibbing Daily Tribune* (March 18, 2004). Reprinted by permission of the author.

"Apostrophe 's': We'll Add It to Everything" by Jamesetta Walker from the *Clarion Ledger* (February 26, 2006). Reprinted by permission of the author.

Acknowledgments for borrowed material continue on p. viii.

Library of Congress Cataloging-in-Publication Data
Dunn, Patricia A.
    Grammar rants : how a backstage tour of writing complaints can help students make informed, savvy choices about their writing / Patricia A. Dunn and Ken Lindblom.
        p. cm.
    Includes bibliographical references and index.
    ISBN-13: 978-0-86709-605-7
    ISBN-10: 0-86709-605-5
    1. English language—Grammar—Study and teaching. 2. English language—Rhetoric—Study and teaching. 3. English language—Usage.   I. Lindblom, Ken. II. Title.

PE1112.D86 2011
428—dc22   2011005689

Editors: Charles I. Schuster and Lisa Luedeke
Production: Vicki Kasabian
Cover design: Matthew Simmons
Typesetter: Kim Arney
Manufacturing: Steve Bernier

Printed in the United States of America on acid-free paper
15 14 13 12 11 VP 1 2 3 4 5

For our mothers,
Rita B. Dunn and Anne Russell,
who raised us to speak well
and not to take any guff from anyone.

Contents

Introduction
What Is a Grammar Rant?

Judging the Judges

Every day, in private conversations, letters to editors, journal articles, and advice columns, people complain about grammar. They love to hate the bad grammar of others. These are the *grammar ranters*, and they claim to be distressed or confused by the tiniest of mistakes:

> The run-on sentence is thus the very picture of intellectual hiatus.
>
> —*Peter Kalkavage (1998)*

> A run-on sentence (also known as a comma splice) blurs connections and breeds confusion.
>
> —*David H. Lynn (1993)*

> I believe people aren't as concerned with correct grammar or punctuation just as much as they are not concerned with morals and our dress anymore.
>
> —*Gerry Cain (qtd. in Walker 2006)*

Secretly, however, grammar ranters may be tickled by the opportunity to point out an error, and, though claiming confusion, they are rarely confused by it. From this position of Innocent Victim of Improper English, they can attack the speaker or writer who produced the error, thereby elevating themselves as more educated, more intelligent, even more moral than the offender making the error. A rant can be a college student's blog (e.g., "I Judge You When You Use Bad Grammar"), a website (e.g., "The Apostrophe Protection Society"), or a syndicated column. Where can rants be found? In newspaper editorials, in YouTube videos, in websites about English grammar, or on bulletin boards. (For a quick sample, type the words *appalling grammar* in any Internet search engine. Hit enter, and stand back!) They may also erupt at any time in faculty lounges or polite dinner-party conversations.

This book is not an attack on proper grammar. Nor is it a suggestion that standards in writing or speaking should be lowered. Quite the contrary: language is a rich, multifaceted tool for effective communication, and to use it well, writers and speakers must attend to conventions of genre, expectations of audience, organization, use of evidence, and much, much more. To help students develop these skills, however, teachers cannot make traditional grammar instruction the center of their lessons.

The problem with grammar rants is that they increase pressure on writing instructors to cover grammar traditionally—even if teaching grammar in conventional ways doesn't help students write or speak better, as a great deal of research shows (see, for example, Graham and Perin 2007). However, we believe exposing students to grammar rants can be an effective way of helping them actually learn more about grammar, writing, reading, and critical thinking.

A grammar rant is a published complaint about other people's language use, but it is rarely about sophisticated aspects of writing. It does not address originality, subject matter, organization, or creativity. It does not address effectiveness of argument, accuracy of evidence, quality of support for claims, appeal to particular readers, effective or ineffective use of emotions or figures of speech. Most rants do not even focus on grammar per se, but rather on minute stylistic features, such as the placement of a comma or an apostrophe. The level of a grammar ranter's outrage is often in inverse proportion to the level of the error's importance in the overall meaning of the piece. Readers may quietly accept an outrageous, unsupported, or even racist or misogynous claim by a writer, but they will be *appalled* (a frequently used adjective) or rendered *aghast* by the way that writer formed a plural or possessive noun. You'd think, and some ranters even claim, that using nonstandardized grammar will lead to the downfall of civilization!

Many grammar rants complain that the writing is not "clear." Double negatives, which rarely confuse anyone in real life, are described as utterly

Favorite words or phrases of grammar ranters: *appalled, aghast, shocked, dismayed, decline of Western civilization.*

Question: What punctuation mark is used more frequently in grammar rants than almost anywhere else? Answer: The exclamation point. (Isn't that appalling?!!!)

confounding, and misplaced commas inspire dumbfoundedness from some otherwise highly intelligent people. This lack-of-clarity complaint, however, sometimes parades as a neutral stand-in for a much more ominous critique of writers who make such errors.

As Joseph Williams has demonstrated in his well-known 1981 scholarship, correctness is often a function of who is writing what for whom: who the reader is, who the writer is, and the power difference between them. Williams has shown that if the writer is perceived to have a lower status than the reader, for example, a teacher reading a student's paper, then the reader will expect to find—and proceed to find aplenty—items to be corrected. On the other hand, if the writer has a higher status than a reader, for example, the writer of a published handbook on style, the reader of that handbook is far less likely to expect error, to look for it, or even to literally see it when it is there. Williams calls this effect "the phenomenology of error." That is, the finding of error is, to some extent, a function of the relationship between reader and writer. No one is claiming here that writers never make mistakes or that readers are totally imagining errors. But the social status of both reader and writer plays into the perception of error far, far more often than most grammar ranters acknowledge. If students are to have a realistic perception of real-world writing, they need to be brought in on this phenomenon.

Grammar rants frequently turn out to be really about those whose language is being critiqued. Looking beneath the surface, one can discover grammar ranters making serious and damaging implications about the moral character or intelligence of the writers attacked for using incorrect grammar. Using grammar rants as texts in writing classes can raise students' awareness of real-world grammatical issues and can strengthen their textual analysis and critical thinking skills. Furthermore, because students are not the targets of the rants, they won't feel personally attacked and will thus be more open to learning the important information about grammar and language that can be gleaned from grammar rants.

Why Analyze Grammar Rants?

We seek to help instructors take student writers on a backstage tour of the claims made in grammar rants and to convince teachers *to let students in on* the dubious advice, questionable assumptions, and prejudicial remarks evident in many public complaints about grammar. The intrigue of analysis and the drama of human conflict can draw students into a piece they are reading

Edgar Schuster has a great double-negative test in his book, *Breaking the Rules: Liberating Writers Through Innovative Writing Instruction* (2003). He suggests asking one student to pretend she is standing at a soda machine, but that she doesn't have change for it. She should ask several other students if they have change. Each student should say in response, "I don't have no change." In no instance has any student standing at the soda machine ever been confused and thought the student actually had change, even though many people claim that a double negative is really a positive.

Phenomenology is the idea that reality is shaped by people's perceptions of it. Joseph Williams makes the point that sometimes an error exists only because a powerful reader *believes* the error exists. Writers writing to readers who are more powerful than they are must be ready to be held responsible for errors they didn't even actually make. (If *this* hasn't led to the decline of civilization, what will?!)

or writing, helping them focus on those other important aspects of the text. Rather than be intimidated or shamed by the implications present in these essays, news stories, or blogs, student writers should investigate the validity of the grammar advice presented, engage in ongoing debates about grammar, and critically examine the assumptions implied about language and people.

Student writers are used to having their writing assessed, commented upon, and judged. At least some of the time, they should judge the judges. As teachers guide their students through close readings of grammar rants, young writers may feel more control over the choices they make about language use, and they'll learn a great deal about writing. From grammar rant analysis, students will learn:

- how different genres (news features, editorials, blogs, and syndicated columns) have different conventions;
- how to anticipate readers' reactions to comma or spelling errors;
- how symbols, metaphors, word choice, inference, irony, and tone add to meaning;
- how writers choose words for the connotations they spark in readers' minds;
- how word association can turn mistake-makers into sinners and those-who-notice-such-things into saints;
- how to research grammar rules in a variety of handbooks and other professional sources to determine the extent to which grammar ranters are right;
- how to pose critical questions about grammar ranters' motives (Is this essay really all about lack of clarity?) and society's values (Do I accept the assumed values here?).

Students may come away with more knowledge about grammar, writing, and reading than many ranters possess. All this analysis will build their confidence, an ingredient needed for the deep revisions and multiple editings most good writers must perform. As they read grammar rants carefully, students can also develop a healthy, informed skepticism about what they read.

Using This Book

In our five chapters, we offer background information and close readings of many grammar rants, separated by topic: Chapter 1: rants on grammar and morality; Chapter 2: rants on grammar and intelligence; Chapter 3: rants on spelling; Chapter 4: rants on texting language; Chapter 5: rants on pronouns, apostrophes, run-on sentences, comma splices, sentence fragments, and other situations we refer to as "grammar traps." We also include several "marked-up" rants, with our comments and questions in the margins. Instructors can then model this analysis for their students, posing critical questions about grammar ranters' claims and evidence. In each chapter, we also reprint published grammar rants and suggest several lessons that can be used as is or modified according to students' needs. By using or adapting the questions, writing tasks, small-group work, and other projects described in these lessons, teachers can empower students to see for themselves the many layers of typical grammar rants, which purport to point out grammar flaws, but which really do so much more.

The grammar rants analyzed in this book reveal some contradictions and hypocrisies in some popular conceptions of grammar that have undue influence on how grammar and writing are taught. Instructors can help students discover some of these contradictions so that they are not misled by bad advice or humiliated by explicit or implicit insults regarding their language practices, or those of their families. Students may also discover that what is deemed correct by one teacher or future supervisor can be seen as an anachronistic faux pas by another. (The generic pronoun *him* is just one example.) Ultimately, we hope this book will help promote what we call "savvy" writing. Savvy writers know the conventions of genre, their own levels of power in each writing situation, and the expectations of their audience. Analyzing grammar rants can heighten the skills necessary for savvy writing.

We Are *Raising* Standards

We are not against "correct grammar." In fact, because so many people with a bit of power claim to be sticklers about grammar, we believe it is doubly important that students proofread carefully any writing projects that will be read by instructors, potential employers, admission committees, and so on. Because some readers relish pointing out other people's mistakes, as we will see, students especially must learn to copyedit their work carefully, with a sophisticated sense of which errors, real or imagined, are most likely to upset which readers, and under what circumstances.

We are also not in favor of lowering standards. In fact, we're for *raising* standards. Students (and instructors) need to go far beyond the low-level trollings for fragments, run-ons, comma splices, apostrophe errors, and the like that still take up too much time and energy in some writing courses today.

If writers, especially novice writers of any age, are told only what they're doing wrong in their writing and are focused only on surface concerns of writing, these writers may do the only thing they know will result in fewer negative comments on their next draft: they will write less. Their essays will become shorter. They will think of themselves as bad writers, and they may write only when they *have* to. They may internalize the larger judgments about their intellect or moral character, judgments lurking in many grammar rants. They may come to think they are bad writers, that their ideas are bad, or even that they are bad people. They may think of themselves as less intelligent or less moral than those who hold the red pens. Some may wish to "better" themselves by learning good grammar, believing (erroneously) that memorizing parts-of-speech nomenclature will lead to good writing. Others may get fed up with the constant attention to trivia and avoid whatever situation puts them in a position of being preached at and criticized for their writing.

Experienced writers, on the other hand, do not take the sticklers as much to heart. They've dealt with enough readers to know that idiosyncratic judgments about grammar will always be with us, and that minor typos and other errors can be handled when they proofread later. Writing takes confidence in self and confidence that readers will take the writing seriously. And experienced writers have an overall confidence about themselves and their writing that allows them to keep going. They've had past success with readers really reading their writing and commenting on their *ideas,* and they write with the confidence needed to shush any imagined grammar sticklers for the time they need to shape their ideas. They push past the finger waggers. They give them cocktails (or hand them a dictionary) and shut them in a back room for a while. Experienced writers do the important work first: they write. They know full well the meticulous editing that needs to be done by someone (a professional copy editor, if they're lucky) before the piece is published. But they don't hyperventilate about proofreading before they've finished getting their ideas out. They don't drop everything to run to a grammar handbook. They write.

Good readers have confidence, too. To become informed, fully-participating, literate citizens, students need to think critically about advertisements, blogs, film reviews, political speeches, and other nonfiction pieces such as editorials, letters to editors, and syndicated or local columns on language use. They need to learn to pose questions about a wide variety of texts and to analyze the anticipated audience, purpose, and tone of the writer or even his or her vested interest in the topic. Analyzing grammar rants in the ways we suggest can enhance this process while also raising language awareness.

Through their imaginative use of our suggestions, instructors should be able to engage students at all levels of writing proficiency—students who may not always write in complete sentences, for example—or students who may not have ever been asked before to analyze assumptions writers seem to make about readers. We have much confidence in students at all levels of placement. We believe that instructors should have high expectations for every student. Although we have great respect for writing instructors, we think some may not have enough confidence in the language knowledge their students already possess or in students' natural intellectual curiosity (which may have been reduced, ironically, by the very "basic lessons in grammar" so many grammar ranters think young writers need).

The sample lessons included are intended to encourage writing instructors to consider alternatives to traditional grammar instruction. This book also gives teachers some of the background they need to speak with authority about hot-button issues in the grammar controversy, to provide facts about grammar, and to model the process of doing rhetorical analyses of published grammar rants. This background knowledge will help those teaching (or taking) writing classes to continue to discover the contradictions and disturbing judgments that so complicate our society's relationship with language practices.

Caveats, Thanks, and Apologies

We are aware that many of the grammar rants we cite may not actually be discussing what most linguists would define as *grammar*: the study of syntax, morphology, structural rules, and so on. Some complaints about "bad grammar" focus on usage or stylistic preferences, not grammar in the strictest sense. However, because this book analyzes what published writers say about "bad grammar" or "proper grammar," we will use the term in the same general sense they do, including rules and syntax, but also usage, punctuation, style, and even spelling.

We are grateful to those writers who generously granted permission for us to reprint their essays in this book. We share their concern about careful language use, and—even when we are taking them to task—we believe their work was written with the best intentions. Our comments on some grammar rants may sound harsh. If our polemical language or snarky comments (made to highlight the drama of grammar rant analysis) offend anyone, we apologize.

We intend our heightened reaction to these grammar rants as a vehicle through which to engage students, bored long ago by grammar trivia, in higher-level language matters. We also intend our analyses as indelicate correctives of the ways in which some grammar ranters have put others down, often unfairly and without any apology.

Grammar ranters' ideas, however, once launched into the public sphere, should be open to scrutiny because they can influence how young writers are taught, how they think of themselves, whether they decide to continue writing, or even whether they decide to stay in school. Grammar rants both reflect and perpetuate society's views of English and the people who use it. Writers and publishers of these rants are responsible for the declarations, claims, and assumptions evident in them, and they should tolerate (even if they do not welcome) active engagement with those declarations, claims, and assumptions.

This book may anger some readers. Although that's not our intention, there is simply no gentle way to report what we found in some of the grammar rants we examined. Our arguments are supported by textual evidence—synthesis, analysis, and direct quotations from grammar rants read, reread, and studied over a number of years. We think instructors (and students) should examine these rants closely, too. If their reading of them differs from ours, so be it: we are happy if we have opened a serious examination or debate regarding what people say about other people's use of language.

Grammar Rants

1

Grammar Rants
and Morality

Background Information

- Those who use good grammar are good people.
- Those who use bad grammar are bad people.

The two statements above are clearly so absurd that most reasonable people reject them outright. However, the connection between grammar and morality is a strong undercurrent in most grammar rants, though it's not always immediately visible. Ranters frequently connect "correct grammar" with goodness and "bad grammar" with evil, though the link may be implied or subliminal, thus increasing its power. Only rarely are ranters rude enough, honest enough, or conscious enough of the connection they're making to state it outright. Most do so through insinuation, allowing metaphor and word connotation to trigger the associations in readers' minds. This unspoken connection is more insidious and harmful to those on the receiving end than are direct statements, which could be more easily recognized for the insults they are, and thus challenged.

One possible reason for bad grammar's association with bad morals is the perceived connection between error and laziness: "Americans are a little lazy with speech" (qtd. in Garrett 2005). People who make mistakes in grammar are often considered to be tasteless, contemptuous of authority,

Some favored words of grammar ranters (when talking about others): *lazy, slovenly, haphazard, sloppy, inconsistent, uneducated, illiterate, illogical.*

Postlapsarian lament: *postlapsarian* means "after the fall," and it refers to the religious belief that once human beings lost the grace of God, they lost their goodness and must struggle to reclaim it. A *postlapsarian lament* is a statement of dismay that people continue to be unworthy of grace. Even grammar ranters who do not claim any religious feeling at all often seem to blame what they consider poor grammar on the basic lack of goodness they see in most people. This is quite an indictment!

We highly recommend reading Edgar Schuster's *Breaking the Rules: Liberating Writers Through Innovative Grammar Instruction* (2003) for the fascinating historical information he provides about grammar instruction.

but most of all, lazy. Perhaps it is the perceived laziness that ranters connect with one of the seven deadly sins in Christianity: sloth. As we'll show, sloth's contemporary name—*laziness*—surfaces in many grammar rants.

Grammar rants typically express the writer's view that language is deteriorating, and with it, the world, the people in it, and their morals. This disappointment with contemporary society as compared with what was apparently a more perfect past is called a *postlapsarian lament*. Common in our society and in grammar rants, the postlapsarian lament includes the belief that the world has been falling from a higher, more moral position, and we all have been in decline since the first great lapse of morals in the Garden of Eden. These laments frequently expand to support the mythical belief that people didn't used to be so lazy, that students used to write better, and that there once was a time in the "good ole days" when everyone dutifully learned a solid, stable, proper grammar and then went on to become clear writers of error-free prose—and more morally upstanding citizens.

Postlapsarian laments about language are so common, they may even be found occasionally in popular entertainment. For example, in one episode of the TV sitcom *Everybody Loves Raymond* called "Homework," Raymond Barone and his mother Marie have a discussion about the English language arts curriculum. When Raymond uses a double negative in the discussion, Marie reacts with horror and then announces that such poor grammar is "the end of civilization!"

Despite the prevalent complaint that grammar instruction used to be better, history teaches us that there was never actually a time when adults were happy about the grammatical knowledge of the younger generation.

Another possible explanation for the emotional venom in many grammar rants and for grammar's frequent association with good and evil in the moral and religious sense lies with Calvinism, one of the beliefs held by some of this country's founders. Calvinists believed in predestination, that people were predestined or "elected" to go to heaven. Earthly wealth and privilege were seen as evidence of future heavenly rewards. Emily Dickinson's poem, "Mine by the Right of the White Election," (1961, 131) is reputed to be about the role wealth plays as an indicator of bliss in the afterlife. By extension, people's obvious lack of earthly wealth, their poverty, may be seen as prima facie evidence that they were not on the invitation list to heaven.

Attitudes connecting language use and morality were common even early in the history of higher education in the United States. As an example, consider Illinois State Normal University, which was one of the first and most influential teachers colleges in the Midwest. Several of the most prominent professors at ISNU frequently associated grammar and spelling with morality and goodness or evil in very direct terms. For example, Albert Stetson, Professor of Composition (1862–1887) said, "It is safe to say that no subject of school study demands more attention in the schools of Illinois today than Spelling, and the true teacher, recognizing this fact, will leave no means untried to correct an almost *universal evil*." Richard Edwards, the University President from 1862 to 1876, said, "When we reflect that the English tongue furnishes in itself a 'liberal education,' and that an unskillful and slovenly use of it is disastrous to any accuracy of thought, we can not otherwise than deeply regret this state of facts. The Normal University considers it a worthy service to do all that is possible to *remedy this evil*" (qtd. in Harmon 1995, 89).

About Thomas Metcalf, Professor of Pedagogy (1862–1894) and perhaps the university's most influential teacher, it was once said, "To him a false pronunciation, a slip in grammar, a mistake in spelling or calculation was a *kind of sin*; a departure from truth and right" (all emphasis is ours; DeGarmo qtd. in Harper 1935, 86). It is not difficult to find other statements like these among other educators at the time. With these sentiments informing the earliest development of teachers in the United States, is it any wonder our attitudes about language still reflect these moral judgments?

> For more information about attitudes about language and the teaching of grade school teachers at ISNU, see Lindblom, Banks, and Quay (2007).

We're not suggesting that people living in the twenty-first century consciously support the belief that "bad grammar" is truly *evil* or are even fully aware that such beliefs existed at all. However, remnants of Calvinism and the history of attitudes of higher educators may be subtly influencing societal beliefs about the rich and poor, and their respective use of language. Our ancestors' connection of earthly privilege to spiritual superiority, and poverty to moral bankruptcy, could partly explain similar ideas today: those in the wealthy or privileged classes tend to speak a dialect of English that is viewed (by those in the wealthy or privileged classes) as "correct," "proper," or "good." Those in poverty or in the lower and working classes tend to speak a dialect of English that is viewed (by the wealthy or privileged classes) as "incorrect," "improper," or "bad," even though linguists have for years explained that those versions of English are just as grammatically "correct" or "valid" as upper-class dialects of English. Through the shards of a judgmental lens, in which being wealthy means being good, it's easier to see why "proper" English is the English dialect spoken by those considered to be "good" people. It would explain why poor or working-class people, some of whom speak a perfectly fine, but not prestigious, version of English, might internalize these assumptions and talk about wanting to improve their

English and thus "better themselves." This lens also explains why those in or near poverty are sometimes viewed as less moral people and treated as such.

The most damaging feature of grammar rants is this insidious linking of the alleged error with evil and the linking of correct sentences with goodness. It's also the feature that most belies ranters' claims that they are merely doing writers the favor of pointing out their errors, in essence "saving" them from the forces of evil. Many grammar sticklers truly believe they are only commenting on "the grammar." They don't consciously intend to attach a morality codicil. The metaphors the sticklers employ to describe editing errors, however, frequently have religious overtones and border on moral condemnations. Writers don't simply produce errors. They "commit" them, like people commit crimes and sins. In fact, errors are still often referred to as "sins" of punctuation. For example, in a short essay that appeared in the online British newspaper, *Peterborough Today*, Ann Molyneux (2006) recounts her search for spelling and grammar errors in her small town's city center. She calls these errors "misdemeanours" (British spelling). The number one problem concerned apostrophes. She refers to this mistake first as a "vice" and later as a "sin." These are metaphors, of course, but they may not be entirely harmless ones. Not surprisingly, there's a grammar book called *Sin and Syntax* (Hale 1999). There's also *The Grammar Bible* (Strumpf and Douglas 1999).

> Grammar books that invoke religion or morality in their titles: *Sin and Syntax* (Hale 1999), *The Grammar Bible* (Strumpf and Douglas 1999), and *The Chortling Bard: Caught'ya! Grammar with a Giggle for High School* (Kiester 1998, 2003). (When do people say "Caught'ya!"?—When they've caught you doing something "wrong.")

Analyzing Grammar Rants with Moral Implications

The more grammar rants we analyze rhetorically, the more moral judgments emerge from them. The laziness critique also surfaces in "Grammar Gaffes," a short piece by staff writer Kristen Garrett, from the (Beaver County and Allegheny) *Times Online*. Garrett interviews a local English teacher who sees the shortcuts in text messaging not as a natural development of language appropriately tailored to this genre of writing, but as laziness, a moral flaw: "It's a sign of how we like to economize things," she said. "It's kind of a form of lazy speech."

As all linguists know, however, languages tend to move toward economy of expression, often considered a *good* thing in communication, and is particularly important in the tiny screens of the text-messaging world. Garrett continues: "Shortcuts and lazy speech have become common in electronic text messaging." The possibility that the genre of text messaging requires a shortened form and has developed its own efficient language to accommodate that form gets reduced to an easy, negative judgment and postlapsarian lament about the deteriorating state of things, complete with finger wagging regarding the sin of sloth. Because most people who use text messaging today are young, they are an easy target. It is frequently those in the younger generation who are accused of being bad writers, lazier and less moral than the adult generation. Garrett's source is quite explicit about text-message writers being "lazy with speech."

In the following snippet, a source quoted by the ranter also doesn't bother with insinuations, but links grammar and morals directly. This grammar rant is typical of the genre in two ways: it is a local columnist writing for a hometown newspaper, and the expert quoted in the piece is a "former teacher and principal." Columnist Jamesetta Walker (2006) is determined to eradicate apostrophes from store names such as "JCPenney's," "Kroger's," and "Wal-Mart's." In a column she writes for the *Clarion Ledger*, this one entitled "Apostrophe 's': We'll Add it to Everything," Walker complains about what she calls "The 'S Factor.'" She writes that an *s* at the end of Wal-Mart or JCPenney is the "possessive that tickles me most." She says that the drugstore she always called "Eckerd's" is "just Eckerd." In her column, she quotes "grammarian Gerry Cain of Ridgeland," a former principal and teacher, who sees this issue as very serious: "I believe people aren't as concerned with correct grammar or punctuation *just as much as they are not concerned with morals* and our dress anymore" (emphasis ours). Walker's column on supposedly unnecessary apostrophes in store names is somewhat humorous (and, as she says, it "tickles" her), but Cain's linking of "correct grammar" with morality is not funny at all.

Another sentence that casually, if less blatantly, links language use and morals comes from conservative commentator Bill O'Reilly. His multiple *if/then* claims here are quite sweeping:

> If a working-class or poor child rejects education, does not learn to speak properly, does not respect just authority and does not understand that having babies at age 14 is a ticket to ruin, then that child's life will likely be tragic. (O'Reilly 2003)

In the column from which this sentence is taken, O'Reilly mostly complains about Eminem, who he thinks "demeans our basic values." But here he lumps not learning "to speak properly" with antisocial, even criminal, behavior that he says will lead to a "tragic" life. Granted, people do tend to judge one another by language use, so speaking in a nonprestigious English may result in listeners forming discriminatory conclusions about the speaker. But is not speaking "properly" really "tragic"? Is not speaking properly a "ticket to ruin" equal to the other behaviors in O'Reilly's copious list, which includes rejecting education, not respecting "just authority," and "having babies at 14"?

It's not just generic "bad grammar" that can bring out the morality police. They can come running with their nightsticks poised when they detect the tiniest specific error. One of the great battlegrounds in the world of grammar rants concerns apostrophes in plurals. Some people get very upset over errors or perceived errors of this type. They get mad at missing apostrophes and mad at excessive ones. People want the precise number of apostrophes they believe is needed, no more, no less. And they don't know or don't care that different grammar books or house style sheets have different views on this issue of correctness.

Outrage occurs when printed punctuation differs from a reader's *perception* of what is correct. One sore point, for example, is what's called the "greengrocers' apostrophe." It gets its name from homemade signs by people selling fruits or vegetables in public markets, signs on which an apostrophe is added to words that should simply have an *s* at the end (*apples* instead of the greengrocers' *apple's*). Here is how Lynne Truss starts her bestseller, *Eats, Shoots & Leaves*:

> Either this will ring bells for you, or it won't. A printed banner has appeared on the concourse of a petrol station near to where I live. "Come inside," it says, "for CD's, VIDEO's, DVD's, and Book's."
>
> If this satanic sprinkling of redundant apostrophes causes no little gasp of horror or quickening of the pulse, you should probably put down this book at once. (2003, 1)

Truss writes this way, of course, for humor. "Satanic sprinkling" is a cute alliteration, and "gasp of horror" a deliberate hyperbole meant to amuse.

However, *satanic sprinkling* and *horror* are words chosen (consciously or not) for their connotations of evil. Lapses in grammar rules are associated with lapses in morality. Janet Maslin of the *New York Times* summarizes Truss' book this way: "that we are far too forgiving of imprecise language and should be more vigilant" (2004). What do people normally forgive? Sin. What are people normally more vigilant about? Crime. For pointing out these lapses in language, Truss is placed by many of her reviewers at the halo-and-wings end of the moral spectrum. Frank McCourt, in his Foreword to *Eats, Shoots & Leaves*, wants to "nominate her [Truss] for sainthood" (2004, xi). He goes on to say that "thousands of English teachers from Maine to Maui will be calling down blessings" on her. The testimonials for the edition that appeared in the United Kingdom mostly acknowledge the wit and humor in the book. But Michael Skapinker from *The Financial Times* goes further, making a direct and explicit connection with religion. His comment is humorous but telling: "Every company meeting should begin with a reading from [*Eats, Shoots & Leaves*], followed by a prayer of thanks for its existence." And Judith Long (2004), praising the book in her column at *Newsday*, calls Truss "the high priestess of punctuation."

Other writers link grammar and morals. Local columnist Dan Bergan, writing for *The Daily Tribune*, exemplifies the typical grammar ranter who critiques those who are already maligned in our society for other reasons. He begins his rant about the misuse of *it's* with these two paragraphs. He's describing where he saw a billboard with an error, but in his prose we also see clear disapproval not only of the sign, but of what it is advertising: Northern Lights Casino, which is also paying for the sign. Bergan also seems to disapprove of casinos in general (the full column appears in Lesson 1 at the end of this chapter):

> So what do you figure bad grammar is worth to the Northern Lights Casino? By my calculation anywhere from $250–800 each month, depending on the particulars of their contract with Lamar Sign Company. And we're talking a BIG sign here, folks—a full-size billboard ad placed right in downtown Aitkin, Minn.
>
> Traffic heading north on Highway 169 encounters one last temptation as it exits the city, the allure of yet another Minnesota casino. A huge billboard on the west side of the road hints at the fun and potential winnings that can be yours with a visit to Northern Lights Casino near Walker. However, wealth and amusement are not all that can be yours. Prandial pleasure awaits. Your gourmet palate can be sated at the casino restaurant that promises "Dining at it's finest." (Bergan 2004, 1)

Bergan builds his entire column around the apostrophe error in *its*, something he can point to as being unequivocally wrong and printed clearly in a grammar book as such. Paying for a sign that has a spelling error in it can also be viewed as a kind of sin in our capitalistic society: a waste of money. But there are hints that the extra apostrophe is not the only sin, not the only excess to which Bergan objects.

He depicts the casino in language inviting parallels with evil. He introduces the casino sign as the "last temptation" drivers see as they leave town. He chooses words such as *allure* and *hints at*, as if a casino is luring innocent drivers with promises of "fun and potential winnings," "pleasure," "wealth and amusement," and a "sated" palate. This description, with its mini-allegory about alluring temptations and promises, suggests unwholesome pleasures (hedonism) and at least one sin (gluttony). The last sentence in that paragraph spotlights the offending error, "Dining at it's finest," connecting the improper grammar with the improper behavior Bergan may believe goes on at casinos. Casinos, to some people, are by definition associated with sinners, and in Bergan's rant, poor language use appears to be more proof of their immorality. All this has implications for language use, social class, and moral judgment.

As Jackson Lears points out in his 2003 book, *Something for Nothing: Luck in America*, gambling has always been a highly controversial issue in America. Lears describes two conflicting views of success in early America: one associated with luck and separated from the moral worthiness of the successful person; the other assumes an ordered universe where the morally worthy are rewarded with earthly success (2–3).

This latter view to success, "where earthly rewards match ethical merits" (3), is a convenient one for the rich and well-off segments of society. They are not merely lucky: they deserve their comfort. This self-satisfaction is reminiscent of the Calvinist belief that a person's earthly affluence is an outward sign of that person's moral affluence. Lears writes, "Prosperity itself came to seem a sign of God's blessing—at least to the more affluent" (2003, 3).

Further, as "earthly rewards" and "ethical merits" became more tightly linked, it was even more critical for the upper classes to draw a distinction between the risk taking involved in Wall Street business ventures and the risk taking involved in more pedestrian forms of gambling. Therefore, as Lears points out, only certain kinds of risk taking would be condemned. It was important that earthly affluence be linked with merit and goodness, not with luck or grace. In fact, Lears argues that the similarity of the two types of risk—casino "gambling" and stock market "investing"—made it even more imperative that sharp distinctions be drawn between them. Much of the present-day moralizing over casino gaming risk may be a remnant of age-old efforts to distinguish it from Wall Street investment risk, which, if it pays off, can be more easily seen as a successful business venture, not a lucky break. Moreover, the recipient of this windfall can more easily be seen as being rewarded for inherent moral virtues, not beholden to fortune for good luck.

What does all this have to do with grammar? This foray into old Puritan values surrounding wealth and worthiness may explain some of Bergan's intensity of emotion over the misspelled word in the billboard for Northern Lights Casino. The spelling error may represent for him—subliminally no doubt—a sin emblematic of what working-class risk taking represents to risk takers in the upper classes. Any risky enterprise open to luck or chance casts a similar shadow on all gambling, no matter what it is called. If casino gambling is constructed as an occupation of the foolish or immoral, Wall Street gambling can more easily be distanced from it and seen as a legitimate business of the smarter, morally superior set.

Grammar enters the equation labeled with the same class-based judgments. Just as remnants of Calvinism reward the wealthy further with unspoken admiration for their assumed moral superiority, the language spoken by the wealthy is also seen as better, more proper, than the language spoken by those in or near poverty. The former group speaks "good English." The latter group speaks "bad English." Everyone in both groups, save for a radical few, recommends that poor people attempt to better themselves by speaking good English—and they should stay out of those casinos. (Please see our marked-up version of Bergan's grammar rant, right before lessons near the end of this chapter.)

The many examples of grammar rants we cite in this chapter show that the extent of moral outrage over a trivial proofreading error often far exceeds the error's importance. Why do people get so upset? Perhaps the ranters feel so powerless to speak out about the many larger moral atrocities in our world that they pick something more manageable and more seemingly objective. Real moral lapses do not trigger the number or intensity of outcries as will a stray apostrophe on a plural. What to do about very significant social issues seems so enormous, so impossible for one individual to tackle, that she may turn to something more tangible and correctable. The laws governing the moral and ethical morass surrounding foreign wars so exceed people's ability to sort them out on their own that they may choose instead to rant on a grammar rule they can look up and authoritatively report to us. They can be judge and jury over the offending writer, knowing the press and their readers will cheer their moral clarity.

Why should issues of grammar and morality matter to those who teach writing? They matter because attitudes about language use are within our purview as instructors. Making moral judgments about people based upon the kind of English they use or deviations they make from standardized English is logically flawed (philosophically and grammatically) and perpetuates prejudice. All these moral imperatives bound up with grammar and language use may confuse learners about language and may introduce social and psychological factors into what should be more objective content.

When adults (including teachers and parents) respond to student writing primarily by nabbing them for their errors, we are participating in a long tradition of accusation and contempt. When students make errors in their writing or speaking, it does not make them bad people. It makes them learners. In fact, many issues of language are situational, and what counts as correct depends upon the intended audience, the genre, and the content of the communication. There are rights and wrong in language use, but they are not as black and white as most grammar ranters make it appear, and the moral implications, often related to race and class, are simply inappropriate. Instructors and students need to know this so they don't perpetuate these prejudices or allow the moralizing of those ignorant of (or uninterested in) the true complexities of language to beat them down. By helping students become more critical of commonly expressed but inappropriate attitudes about language, we can help them make more informed and less emotionally and morally vexed decisions about their own communication.

As teachers of future English teachers, we work with those who are just beginning the process of becoming certified. Every year we are surprised by some students who include their pleasure in correcting other people's grammar as a reason for wanting to become an English teacher. Correcting grammar is ultimately the job of a copy editor (and a crucial job it is!), not an English teacher. We fear that those students who enjoy correcting really enjoy feeling morally superior to those around them. Otherwise perfectly pleasant, bright, and wonderful people can harbor this unpleasant quality. Are they really just insecure about themselves? Are they simply mimicking the behavior of older adults they admire? Whatever the reason, we believe that the process of correction is often more about the corrector's need than the correctee's. Attuning ourselves and our students to the moral problems associated with good grammar can help all of us eliminate this unproductive approach to the teaching of writing and speaking.

In the next section, following a marked-up grammar rant, we propose two lessons designed to build students' reading and critical thinking skills, draw their attention to language use, and help them recognize and question potentially harmful moral judgments grammar ranters seem to make about other writers.

Marked-Up Grammar Rant

Next, we demonstrate how we "mark up" grammar rants (highlight words and phrases and comment on them). We also include two lessons instructors may use as is or adapt as they see fit.

"Gramme(a)r: Using *Its* and *It's*"*

by Dan Bergan

The Daily Tribune (March 18, 2004)

So what do you figure bad grammar is **worth** to the Northern Lights Casino? By my **calculation** anywhere from $250–800 each month, depending on the particulars of their contract with Lamar Sign Company. And we're talking a BIG sign here, folks—a full-size billboard ad placed right in downtown Aitkin, Minn.

Traffic headed north on Highway 169 encounters one last ***temptation*** as it exits the city, the ***allure*** of yet another Minnesota casino. A huge billboard on the west side of the road hints at the ***fun and potential winnings*** that can be yours with a visit to Northern Lights Casino near Walker. However, ***wealth and amusement*** are not all that can be yours. ***Prandial pleasure*** awaits. Your ***gourmet palate can be sated*** at the casino restaurant that ***promises*** "Dining at it's finest."

Read the quote once more. "Dining at it's finest." Again, as intimated by my opening, I do not know to the **penny** exactly what that billboard in Aitkin **costs** Northern Lights, minimally—based on my research—**$250 monthly**. But whatever the **cost**, they're **spending** lots of **money** on a mistake.

Technically, this second sentence is a fragment. It answers the question raised in the first paragraph, so it's clearly a deliberate or stylistic fragment. But grammar ranters should probably be extra careful about deviating from what other ranters consider "rules."

Note that in this paragraph, Bergan seems to be blaming Lamar Sign Company for the mistake he describes in the third paragraph: *it's* for *its*.

Note the phrase, "yet another Minnesota casino." What can we infer about Bergan's attitude toward casinos in general? How is "yet another Minnesota casino" different from "a Minnesota casino"? (He could have said, "yet another billboard," or "yet another sign company.")

The **bold** words have to do with money.

The writer makes money the focus of three paragraphs: the first, the third, and the last. It's hard to say why he's focused on that. Perhaps wasting money is a kind of a sin in our society.

The ***bold italic*** words have links with moral or religious themes, many associated with alleged promises made by the devil: *temptation, allure, fun and potential winnings, wealth and amusement,* and *promises. Prandial* means having to do with meals. So *prandial pleasure* and *gourmet palate can be sated* are phrases associated with gluttony, one of the seven deadly sins. *Winnings* and *wealth* may be associated with greed, another deadly sin. If this religious/moral interpretation seems like a stretch, note that later in this grammar rant, Bergan specifically mentions Milton's *Paradise Lost*, a classic text that has Lucifer as a main character.

My initial column on Jan. 15 dealt with case forms of pronouns, which simply means that pronouns signal different functions in a sentence by different spellings—case forms. For instance, *he* signals the nominative case of that particular pronoun, which means that form will be used primarily as a subject (He won the game). On the other hand, *him* signals objective case, which simply means that normally that form will be used as the object, or receiver of the action—of a verb (The girl saw him). Pronouns, also, indicate possession, ownership of something, and signal that relationship with a different case form, in this instance *his* (That is his book).

The personal pronoun only has two forms—*it* and *its*. The *it* form serves as both nominative and objective case (Did you enjoy the movie? It was entertaining: I enjoyed it greatly). Add the *s*, and you get the possessive form *its*, which is intended to signal ownership or possession. Thus, you would correctly say "The table had lost one of its legs." Or, "**The Passion of Christ** delivers its message graphically."

Again, if it looks like we're forcing the religion/grammar connection, note this blatant example.

Whereas nouns signal possessive case with an apostrophe and usually an added *s*—such as dog's collar or man's shirt or ship's mast—pronouns have their own special spellings—case forms—to signal the ownership, avoiding the necessity of the apostrophe. So the correct possessive is *his*, not *hi's*; or *hers*, never *her's*; or *theirs*, never *their's*; or *yours*, never *your's*; or *ours*, never *our's*.

What about *someone's*?

So, too, with *its*. Simply add the *s* to create the possessive form. Add an additional apostrophe, as Northern Lights Casino did, and you create an entirely new word, namely the contraction *it is*. In effect, the casino advertised a gourmet experience "at it is finest"—pure nonsense. By making those two little words, Northern Lights **committed**, in the words of noted grammarian John B. Bremner, "the most sickening example of literary ignorance" that exists.

Notice that in this paragraph, Bergan is no longer blaming Lamar Sign Company for the mistake, or even flesh and blood human beings. Now it is *the casino* that "committed" the error. How is "Northern Lights committed" different from "The sign makers made a mistake"?

That "sickening example," however, would have been considered correct usage in the 17th century when *it's* was considered the acceptable possessive form. Read parts of **John Milton's Paradise Lost** or the journals of Lewis and Clark to find numerous examples of such usage. However, since the early 19th century the added apostrophe has been frowned upon and is now considered verboten.

Thus, remind yourself of a simple rule: every time you write *it's*, say to yourself "*It is*," and you won't be advertising—or **paying for**—your ignorance, unlike a certain nearby casino.

TEST YOURSELF—CORRECT OR WRONG?

1. The fault was solely her's.
2. One fawn lost its way in the forest.
3. Theirs was a good idea from the onset.
4. No doubt that its the correct procedure.
5. The message lost its meaning in translation.
6. A dress of her's had mistakenly been cleaned.
7. His left skate lost it's edge on the concrete.
8. The grand prize was our's to claim.
9. It's that time of year—false spring.

(1) w (2) c (3) c (4) w (5) c (6) w (7) w (8) w (9) c

Count how many times the word *casino* is used. Note how the casino is now advertising itself, paying for the ad, and revealing its ignorance.

Many grammar rants end with a quiz like this, where there's a right and a wrong answer for everything.

Note that the essay part of this piece ends with a jab at the casino. (One way to emphasize something is to end with it.) Is the point of the rant about grammar or really about casinos?

The title of this grammar rant leads us to believe it will be mostly about the grammar error of using *it's* instead of *its*. However, the first two paragraphs focus exclusively on the allure of the casino. There are many words and phrases that have religious or moral overtones, thus linking the grammar error with the negative moral judgments the writer seems to be making about casinos in general.

Key

Bold italics = Words or phrases connected with morals or religion

Bold = Words or phrases connected with money

* Words used as words have been italicized in this version.

Lesson 1

Objectives

Students will:

- identify inferences in arguments about language, distinguishing between denotation and connotation
- think critically about writers' language choices and implied attitudes and judgments about people's character

Materials

- Blackboard (or overhead projector, or projection)
- Handout: Connotations, Word Choice, and Implications (p. 17)

Procedures

1. Begin with this motivation, or five-minute warm-up for the lesson:

   Write *Its* and *It's* in giant letters on blackboard, whiteboard, or projection, with the following explanation:

   It's = *it is*, as in "It's a nice day." (It is a nice day.)

   Its = shows possession (when something belongs to it); as in, "The diamond lost its luster."

   Ask the class: "Have any of you ever seen an *it's/its* error or made it yourself? How *do* people get those two words mixed up?" Write students' answers on the board and discuss them.
   Possible answers:

   - The words are very similar.
   - You can't hear the difference in the words in oral conversation; you can only see the difference in the written words.
   - Sometimes people write quickly and get it wrong the first time and then don't proofread or miss it when they proofread.
   - Possession is almost always shown by using an *'s*, and this is a rare exception.

2. Explain: "There's a newspaper columnist named Dan Bergan who quotes grammar expert John B. Bremner, who says that getting these two words mixed up is 'the most sickening example of literary ignorance' that exists." (You could write that quotation on the board, too.)

   Ask the students: "When people usually use the word *sickening*, what kinds of things are they usually talking about? What kinds of behaviors would you consider *sickening*?" List a few of their answers on the board. (Answers will vary, but *sickening* typically describes spoiled food, tragedies, truly disgusting behavior, heinous crimes, etc.)

3. Tell the students that using a word like *sickening* to describe a minor grammar error implies that the minor error is as bad as the things on the list they generated. This implication is called a *connotation*. It is not stated directly, but rather it is suggested without being said outright. Ask students: "Do you agree with John B. Bremner that the *its/it's* error is 'the most sickening example of literary ignorance'? Why or why not?" Discuss briefly.

4. Tell students, "Today we're going to see some other people's reactions to grammar errors and see if we can figure out why they have the reactions they do. In the following excerpts or short readings, writers use words that have powerful *connotations*; that is, meanings that go beyond the words' literal meaning. A word with connotations has *baggage*, and in these cases, they make judgments about people's moral or ethical character. We will discuss whether you agree with these authors about what grammar errors really mean about the people who make them."

5. Distribute handout: Connotations, Word Choice, and Implications.

6. Discuss.

7. Follow-up in-class writing assignment: Ms. Molyneux implies that writers who misuse apostrophes are committing crimes against the public (see handout on p. 17). Write a short paragraph that does one of the following (don't take this assignment *too* seriously!).

   a. Write up the charges against the writers Ms. Molyneux accuses. Include a description of why this "crime" is so bad and what you believe the sentence for the "crime" should be.

   b. Consider that Ms. Molyneux, in judging the moral character of writers who have made a minor grammar error as guilty of a crime, is herself guilty of judging others harshly. Write up charges against her, describe the severity of her "crime," and what you believe the sentence against her should be.

8. Follow-up homework assignment: As you go home today, try to find grammar errors of any kind on street signs (store notices, handwritten notes or signs, announcements, road signs, advertisements). How many people do you think notice such errors? Why do you think the writers of those errors might have made those mistakes? What do you think Mr. Bergan, Mr. Bremner, or Ms. Molyneux would think about those errors?

Handout: CONNOTATIONS, WORD CHOICE, AND IMPLICATIONS

Notice the difference between these two sentences:

My brother says he returned my laptop.

My brother claims he returned my laptop.

What does *claims* imply that *says* does not (unless *says* is deliberately stressed)? Notice the difference between these two sentences:

That woman is a legislator.

That woman is a politician.

Let's say these two sentences are describing the same woman with the same job in government service. Do you think she'd rather be described as a *legislator* or as a *politician*? What does *politician* imply that *legislator* does not? *Claims* and *politician* come with negative connotations. *Says* and *legislator* are a bit more neutral. They denote meaning, but words with powerful connotations, like *claims* and *politician*, can have powerful effects on readers, almost without readers noticing.

Connotations in Grammar Rants

Read the passage below, an excerpt from Ann Molyneux's article ("Duz It Relly Mater If We Cant Spel Properly?") in an online British newspaper, *Peterborough Today*, on November 22, 2006. In her article, she relates how she walked around her town's city center (she spells it *centre*, the British spelling) looking for grammar errors on signs. Here are a few of her early paragraphs, which are very short because this is a news article and short paragraphs are a convention of that genre. As you read, circle any words that you think might have negative connotations:

In Peterborough city centre, the streets are littered with grammatical errors and misspellings likely to raise the hackles of anyone interested in the correct use of the English language.

I spent an hour wandering around, and even though I had my eyes peeled for misdemeanours, they were all in public places and fairly easy to spot.

The number one vice appears to be the misuse of apostrophes. Among the errors I uncovered were a notice on a market stall selling "girl's real leather jackets."

If you took this literally, it would refer to just one girl, rather than girls in general. Of course, the number one sin is when people use an apostrophe in plurals, such as when they write "toy's" or "carrot's."

Answer Key for Handout

Notice *littered*, *misdemeanours* (British spelling), *vice*, and *sin*. These words have connotations. They're linked with trash or garbage (*littered*), crime (*misdemeanor*), bad behavior (*vice*), and moral corruption (*sin*). Exaggeration can be humorous, and these words were probably chosen for that purpose. Linking grammar errors with crimes, bad behavior, and sins, however, can have powerful subconscious, possibly harmful implications. Someone might also notice that the writer has inserted the period *outside* the quotations. That's the British convention. It's less obvious why the writer put "*were* a notice." That might be an example of Hartmann's "Law of Prescriptivist Grammar" (Chivers 2009), which holds that those who rant about other people's grammar errors inevitably make one of their own.

Lesson 2

Objectives

Students will:

- read for more subtle inferences
- read critically for implied connections between grammar and morality
- understand one explanation for how possessive pronouns are formed in standard(ized) English

Materials

- Blackboard or whiteboard, overhead, or projection
- Handout: Worksheet on Bergan's Grammar Rant (p. 22)
- Paper

Procedures

1. Begin with this motivation, or five-minute warm-up for the lesson. Write on the board, overhead, or projection: "If you use good grammar, you're a good person. If you use bad grammar, you're a bad person."

   Ask students: "What do you think of these statements? Have you ever felt ashamed or 'bad' if someone corrects your grammar? Why or why not?" Discuss briefly.

Then give more background: "Although these might seem like ridiculous statements, many people who complain about other people's grammar manage to link the grammar error with bad, even immoral, behavior. Here's what an English teacher from Pennsylvania said to a staff writer at a local newspaper: 'Americans are a little lazy with speech' (quoted in Garrett 2005).

"Laziness may not seem like such a terrible thing, but an ancient word for laziness—*sloth*—was one of the seven deadly sins, along with others such as gluttony (overeating) and greed. Today, we're going to read a grammar rant closely and see if we can detect any subtle, or barely hidden, links between grammar errors and judgments about morality."

2. Briefly define these vocabulary words: *prandial* (meal related), *intimated, sated, gourmet, verboten*. Then read, or have students read, Dan Bergan's essay. (See also our marked-up version of Bergan's rant earlier in this chapter.)

3. Distribute the worksheet on Bergan's grammar rant. Have students do the work, and then discuss their answers either in a teacher-led, open discussion or in small groups. Or, start them off, modeling the process in an open discussion and then let them continue discussing their answers in small groups or pairs, finishing up with groups reporting back to the class.

"Gramme(a)r: Using *Its* and *It's*"*

by Dan Bergan
The Daily Tribune (March 18, 2004)

So what do you figure bad grammar is worth to the Northern Lights Casino? By my calculation anywhere from $250–800 each month, depending on the particulars of their contract with Lamar Sign Company. And we're talking a BIG sign here, folks—a full-size billboard ad placed right in downtown Aitkin, Minn.

Traffic headed north on Highway 169 encounters one last temptation as it exits the city, the allure of yet another Minnesota casino. A huge billboard on the west side of the road hints at the fun and potential winnings that can be yours with a visit to Northern Lights Casino near Walker. However, wealth and amusement are not all that can be yours. Prandial pleasure awaits. Your gourmet palate can be sated at the casino restaurant that promises "Dining at it's finest."

Read the quote once more. "Dining at it's finest." Again, as intimated by my opening, I do not know to the penny exactly what that billboard in Aitkin costs

Northern Lights, minimally—based on my research—$250 monthly. But whatever the cost, they're spending lots of money on a mistake.

My initial column on Jan. 15 dealt with case forms of pronouns, which simply means that pronouns signal different functions in a sentence by different spellings—case forms. For instance, *he* signals the nominative case of that particular pronoun, which means that form will be used primarily as a subject (He won the game). On the other hand, *him* signals objective case, which simply means that normally that form will be used as the object, or receiver of the action—of a verb (The girl saw him). Pronouns, also, indicate possession, ownership of something, and signal that relationship with a different case form, in this instance *his* (That is his book).

The personal pronoun only has two forms—*it* and *its*. The *it* form serves as both nominative and objective case (Did you enjoy the movie? It was entertaining: I enjoyed it greatly). Add the *s*, and you get the possessive form *its*, which is intended to signal ownership or possession. Thus, you would correctly say "The table had lost one of its legs." Or, "The Passion of Christ delivers its message graphically."

Whereas nouns signal possessive case with an apostrophe and usually an added *s*—such as dog's collar or man's shirt or ship's mast—pronouns have their own special spellings—case forms—to signal the ownership, avoiding the necessity of the apostrophe. So the correct possessive is *his*, not *hi's*; or *hers*, never *her's*; or *theirs*, never *their's*; or *yours*, never *your's*; or *ours*, never *our's*.

So, too, with *its*. Simply add the *s* to create the possessive form. Add an additional apostrophe, as Northern Lights Casino did, and you create an entirely new word, namely the contraction *it is*. In effect, the casino advertised a gourmet experience "at it is finest"—pure nonsense. By making those two little words, Northern Lights committed, in the words of noted grammarian John B. Bremner, "the most sickening example of literary ignorance" that exists.

That "sickening example," however, would have been considered correct usage in the 17th century when *it's* was considered the acceptable possessive form. Read parts of John Milton's *Paradise Lost* or the journals of Lewis and Clark to find numerous examples of such usage. However, since the early 19th century the added apostrophe has been frowned upon and is now considered verboten.

Thus, remind yourself of a simple rule: every time you write *it's*, say to yourself "*It is*," and you won't be advertising—or paying for—your ignorance, unlike a certain nearby casino.

Test Yourself—Correct or Wrong?

1. The fault was solely her's.
2. One fawn lost its way in the forest.
3. Theirs was a good idea from the onset.
4. No doubt that it's the correct procedure.
5. The message lost its meaning in translation.
6. A dress of her's had mistakenly been cleaned.
7. His left skate lost it's edge on the concrete.
8. The grand prize was our's to claim.
9. It's that time of year—false spring.

w (2) c (3) c (4) w (5) c (6) w (7) w (8) w (9) c

* *Words used as words have been italicized in this version.*

WORKSHEET ON BERGAN'S GRAMMAR RANT

1. Examine these two sentences. First, Bergan's original sentence:

   Traffic headed north on Highway 169 encounters one last temptation as it exits the city, *the allure of yet another Minnesota casino*. [our emphasis]

   And then this one:

   Traffic headed north on Highway 169 encounters one last temptation as it exits the city, *an advertisement for a Minnesota casino*. [our emphasis]

   What's the difference in meaning between "*the allure of yet another* Minnesota casino" and "*an advertisement for* a Minnesota casino"? What does the first phrase connote that the second does not? Why do you say that? Discuss your answers in large or small groups, as directed by your instructor.

2. Notice any words or phrases on Bergan's grammar rant that seem connected in any way to morality or religion. Write a brief comment about how that word or phrase is connected to religion or morality. Discuss your answers in large or small groups, as directed by your instructor.

3. Who does Bergan believe is at fault for the *its/it's* error? What makes you say this?

4. What seems to be Bergan's attitude toward casinos in general? What other words or phrases does he use that make you say this?

5. Follow-up in-class writing assignment: What might be some reasons why a complaint about the *its/it's* error has so many implied connections to religion or morality? Is grammar a moral or religious issue? If yes, why? If no, why are there so many religious or moral overtones in this rant, and the reference to laziness in the statement by the Pennsylvania English teacher, above ("Americans are a little lazy with speech.") ? Do you think grammar and morals should be connected?

6. Follow-up homework assignment: Search the Internet for an article or blog that discusses grammar in a way that uses moral or judgmental language. What words make those connotations? Do you agree or disagree with the author of the piece you have found? Bring a copy of the article or blog and your response to it to class to discuss or hand in.

Answer Key and Discussion Points for Lesson 2

1. Answers will vary, but *allure* has a slightly tainted, even diabolic over-tone. And *yet another* seems to express a frustration on the part of the writer that there are any casinos in Minnesota, let alone "yet another."

2. *Temptation, The Passion of Christ, Paradise Lost,* to name just a few. See the bold italic words pointed out in the marked-up grammar rant earlier in this chapter. Students might need help coming up with words related to temptation, allure, wealth, and so on. They may need reminding that along with sloth, discussed earlier, gluttony is also one of the seven deadly sins.

3. In his first paragraph, Bergan seems to blame Lamar Sign Company for the error. By the end of the essay, he seems to be blaming the casino itself.

4. He doesn't seem to like casinos. He spends almost as much time talking about casinos as he does the *its/it's* error. He uses the word *casino* many times. Yes, he's talking about an ad for casinos, so he does have to use that word occasionally, but he could have focused more on the billboard, the sign company, or ads in general.

5. Answers will vary, but there's a long history in this country of some religions disapproving of gambling. Or, his disapproval could have something to do with the "tempting" nature of the ad, or the references to *prandial pleasures, gourmet palates,* and other associations with gluttony. There are also connotations of greed.

Further Questions and Activities (Optional)

1. Notice all the words on Bergan's rant that have to do with money. (See the bolded words on the marked-up grammar rant earlier in this chapter.) Why so many? What is implied about grammar errors with all these connections to money, laziness, greed, and gambling?

2. Find a fragment. (For example, see the second sentence: *By my calculation anywhere from $250–800 each month, depending on the particulars of their contract with Lamar Sign Company.*) Is it an error or is it deliberate? What makes you think so?

3. Write a hypothetical letter either to Mr. Bergan or to the owners of either the sign company or the casino about the use of *it's* for *its* on their sign. Express your own position on the matter and recommend a solution to the problem, determining who is at fault and who should pay for any required correction to the sign. (In your letter, be careful not to use the wrong *its*!)

2

Grammar and Intelligence

Background Information

As we show in Chapter 1, people make many direct comments or powerful insinuations about writers' morality based on their departures from grammar ranters' ideas of correctness. Ranters also freely remark upon writers' intelligence—or sometimes education or social class—based on their use of an apostrophe, a comma, and so on.

Although today's grammar ranters casually toss out derogatory judgments about people's intelligence or education based on nothing more than the ranter's detection of an error or something they think is an error, the effect of those comments might be quite harmful. If writers or speakers are made to believe that their language choices reflect their intelligence, it's no wonder that many students are reluctant to speak in class or to produce much writing.

It's amazing what conclusions some people will draw based on errors they detect in other people's writing. One error can launch grammar ranters into a diatribe about the end of times. Says Max Clio in his rant in *The Chronicle of Higher Education*: "I am an embedded observer in the decline of Western civilization. At least, that was the distinct sensation that came over me earlier today, while working my way through a pile of student papers" (2003, C2) . Ranters also fault the 1960s, hippies, and free love. They blame the Internet, the media, karaoke, whole language, even gym class, for what they see as a deterioration, not only of language, but of morality and of intelligence or education, as we explore in this chapter.

Grammar ranters complaining about language use often do not provide support for their claims but rely instead on what they believe are shared assumptions within a group (e.g., that language is deteriorating, that teachers who don't correct every error they can find are lazy, that children aren't as smart as they used to be, etc.). Ancient rhetoricians called these shared assumptions—which need not be true—"commonplaces" (Crowley and Hawhee 2009, 20–21). If readers do, indeed, share those commonplaces, writers need not support their claims for their arguments to work.

This is a problem because it allows ignorance to spread rapidly. If writers express attitudes that readers already agree with (or mostly agree with, unless they really think about it), then no proof at all is required; in fact, something that looks like proof can function as powerfully as rigorously conclusive proof—even though it shouldn't.

However, if readers do not share the assumptions of a particular writer, the writer's claims can backfire, making the writer seem misinformed, illogical, naïve, mean-spirited, or even—in extreme cases—bigoted.

> Here are some of the targets of grammar ranters' wrath: the Internet, spell-check programs, hippies, the media, whole language, gym class, famous athletes, and even karaoke!

Analyzing Grammar Rants with Negative Implications About Intelligence

Newspaper columnist Randi Weiner laments the "deterioration of grammar." (See a marked-up version of her complete column at the end of this chapter.) She includes an insinuation about the intelligence of sign makers:

> *Writers, teachers and people who know the difference between "its" and "it's" all have stories about errors they've seen while stopped at a light, standing in line at a gas station, or looking at a board of lunch specials while deliberating between the hamburger or the tuna sandwich.* (2005; our emphasis)

This sentence seems to be less about the confusion these errors allegedly breed and more about how the error functions as a marker of the "people who know the difference." It's the writers and teachers versus the gas station owners and lunch counter workers. While their sandwiches are being made for them, these "people who know the difference" have the leisure to critique the hastily written signs created by people rushing to scribble a lunch

> Some people get a lot of mileage out of correcting errors. A new book describes the story of two men who cross the United States trying to correct errors on 437 signs: *The Great Typo Hunt: Two Friends Changing the World One Correction at a Time* by Jeff Deck and Benjamin D. Herson (2010).

menu or trying to run a gas station. The eaters of those hamburgers or tuna sandwiches can now go home and tell their friends amusing stories about the errors they've seen.

Unlike Randi Weiner and other columnists who write for their local newspaper (and unlike us, too), these sign makers do not have someone working for them who is paid to proofread what they write. Unlike their white-collar critics, they may not be using a word processing program that flags misspellings. These busy sign makers may have only a few minutes before the lunch hour rush to grab a marker, list the specials, and move on to the next task. To their credit, Weiner and her fellow *its/it's* experts do not claim to be confused by the signs they see at gas stations or the corner lunch counter, as some grammar ranters pretend to be. They seem satisfied just knowing that they are right, the sign writers are wrong, and that they, the ones with this impressive knowledge of the difference between a possessive pronoun and a contraction, are proud that they are so good at "resisting the urge to correct grammar" (except behind people's backs). But notice that it is the consumers of other people's services who have the luxury of resisting the urge to correct the signs of those who own or work at these gas stations and lunch counters, providing service to the ones who disapprove of their signs.

The most over-the-top hyperbole about the *its/it's* error comes from *Eats, Shoots & Leaves*. Notice how Lynne Truss states outright that the mistake tells her something about *the writer*, that it is a "signal" about the human being who created the error:

> The confusion of the possessive "its" (no apostrophe) with the contrac-tive "it's" (with apostrophe) is *an unequivocal signal of illiteracy* and sets off a simple Pavlovian "kill" response in the average stickler. (2003, 43; our emphasis)

Truss is exaggerating here for the sake of humor. Still, her judgment of the *its* error being "an unequivocal signal of illiteracy" does seem close to what many grammar ranters say about writers they think are "confused" by the two words. (Or, it may be that people are not "illiterate." They may simply write fast and make a typo.) Truss continues her rant about *it's* and *its*:

> Getting your itses mixed up is the greatest solecism in the world of punc-tuation. No matter that you have a PhD and have read all of Henry James twice. If you still persist in writing, "Good food at it's best", you deserve to be struck by lightning, hacked up on the spot and buried in an unmarked grave. (43–44)

To her credit, and like Randi Weiner, above, Truss does not pretend that "Good food at it's best" is confusing. We are never asked to imagine readers standing around scratching their heads in helpless befuddlement. Instead, her focus is on what punishment should be meted out to the person who dares to write *it's* instead of *its*—because of what she says it tells her about that person. Yes, she's kidding, but at whose expense?

In the previous quotation, Lynne Truss has placed the comma *outside* the quotation mark, after the word *best*. In the United States, the comma would be placed *inside* the quotation mark, but in Britain—where Truss' book was published—the comma should be placed *outside* the quotation mark. As students will discover by reading grammar rants, many of "the rules of correct grammar" are not universal. What counts as "correct" often depends on where you are. Maybe grammar handbooks should have maps in them!

Randi Weiner's rant continues with more anecdotes about people who are compelled to correct grammar on signs they see around town. We're told:

> Brian Monahan, deputy assistant superintendent for North Rockland schools, still remembers his conversation at a local car repair shop that had posted a "Your car serviced while your (sic) sleeping" sign a couple years ago.

Weiner tells us nothing more about this incident, but let's imagine the circumstances in which this conversation took place. Monahan has just driven his car into an open bay of his local repair shop, perhaps to get the oil changed and the car checked out before a trip. His car now in the hands of the mechanic, Monahan proceeds to criticize the language of the person fixing his car.

People who criticize other people's grammar usually imply that the people whose grammar they're critiquing lack some social etiquette or have made some kind of social blunder. Or they imply that people who make a grammar error are stupid. But if what deputy assistant superintendent Monahan told local columnist Randi Weiner is true—that he actually had a conversation at the car repair shop regarding the owner's misspelled sign— we suggest that it is Monahan who is making the social blunder and not being very smart here. We hope the mechanic wasn't so distracted about the grammar error that he forgot to test the brakes carefully!

Weiner also interviews Sam Tupper (pseudonym), a retired English teacher and principal with rigid views of grammar and intelligence and what he sees as a general decline in language. Tupper, writes Weiner, "traces the deterioration of grammar to the 1960s, when what he called the 'era of relevance' invaded the nation's schoolrooms." The reporter does not ask Tupper to support his view that grammar is deteriorating or that the 1960s caused such a thing. Both of them seem to share the same assumption regarding the two claims, a case of commonplace in practice. The article continues by apparently indirectly quoting Tupper about the relationship between grammar and intelligence: *"that those who speak properly are more intelligent than those who don't,* Tupper said" (our emphasis).

Tupper also takes a shot at the "Whole Language movement, which encouraged the youngest children to write long before they were expected to understand the laws of apostrophes, commas, and spelling." This statement is also left uninterrogated by the reporter, as if Tupper's summary of whole language is complete and fair, and as if all informed people would agree with his implication that young children should have to know all "the laws" of punctuation and spelling before they are allowed to write anything. Tupper later calls these "laws" of grammar "rules," and still later, "a lost art form," perhaps even more difficult for young writers to master completely before they are allowed to compose anything. If Tupper's advice on teaching writing were to be followed, children would get the idea that "writing" was nothing more than lessons on apostrophes, commas, and spelling. Who could blame them if they turned to video games?

Tracy Lee Simmons, director of the journalism program at Hillsdale College, also weighs in on how writing and grammar should be taught, and like Tupper, makes a connection between language and intelligence. As does Tupper, Simmons takes a jab at educational trends:

> We can see the damage wrought upon us all by "empowerment" learning—namely, not so much that words fail us, but that we fail words, *the mindful use of which once supplied a fairly reliable key to one's intelligence and culture.* (2000, 48; our emphasis)

For Simmons, too, good grammar apparently equals high intelligence and good breeding, manners, or culture. If Simmons' readers agree with this unfounded assumption, there is no need for him to support this claim with any evidence. So he doesn't bother to provide any.

Simmons tells us that one time in the 1980s, he heard one new-age textbook author claim that writing could be used as a path to self-discovery. He then takes this one speaker's one point to represent everything he sees wrong with writing. He sees "clarity," "concision," and "accuracy" in opposition to creativity, "self-fulfillment," and "political awareness." He reduces all writing pedagogy that doesn't foreground and dwell upon grammar and usage to "a sandal-shod, flannel-clad way of life" (2000, 49).

Many grammar ranters blame video games and social networking sites for what they see as a decline in the intelligence and work ethic of young people. In fact, some scholars believe there is a great deal of intelligence and positive work ethic developed by working on computers—for examples, consult Gee (2007) and Johnson (2005).

Simmons suggests that sometimes "we fail words." For those of us who see language as a tool for creating and sharing meaning, this comment makes little sense. If a carpenter mishits a nail, has the carpenter failed the hammer? What does the hammer care? Turning language into an entity that we could fail, like a disappointed parent, is a form of anthropomorphizing. Some grammar ranters use anthropomorphism to shame people who make language errors. Don't fall for this misplaced guilt. The language is there for *us*, not the other way around.

What is the "empowerment learning" that caused all this "damage" to "concision and clarity"? Simmons blames an amorphous "political awareness" being foisted upon students in a writing class, as if issues of power played no role whatsoever in writing classes before the 1960s: "How did anyone fob off the idea, sometime between the Beatles' first LP and disco, that writing one's language simply and accurately isn't enough for one course?" (2000, 48)

As with Tupper's claims, there is no factual evidence for Simmons' declarations, just the occasional rhetorical question aimed at an audience that no doubt shares his assumptions (the "we" in "We can see the damage"). Writing for *National Review*, Simmons is probably counting on his readers to have the same answers he does to his rhetorical questions. It's only when these statements and questions are encountered by readers who do *not* share his assumptions that his lack of any evidence for his claims shows up in sharp relief. And although he chastises some writing classes for having "a not-always-stated purpose, political awareness"—thus implying that writing classes can and should be free of opinions on social issues—he can't help inserting an opinion of his own on social issues, a jab at a children's book: "*Heather Has Two Mommies* may not provide the best possible artifact of clean prose" (49).

Simmons proposes a solution to all this reputed deterioration of grammar. He says that English composition classes should be taught by foreign language instructors, and he makes this astounding claim: "those who teach foreign languages are, as a rule, among the most acutely intelligent and patient to be found in any institution" (49).

He also seems to hold two opposing views of how difficult all this would be. Early in his essay he says learning how to write is challenging: "Writing well has been a thorny task at all times; the best practitioners of the craft have always borne witness that good writing doesn't come naturally. It's a sweaty, punishing business" (48). Shortly after that statement, however, he says it's all quite simple: "What we need now are folks who can teach the craft of prose, which is a much simpler matter than the theorists would have us believe" (48). Still later, he says, "No drudgery, no learning" (49), and that instruction should be "grindingly serious. While learning to write well can be satisfying, it isn't fun" (49). So which is it? Simple and easy or thorny and serious?

The latter belief is what New York University professor John S. Mayher calls "the castor oil syndrome," the assumption by many people that real learning is difficult and arduous (1990, 52). Such an assumption is convenient for those who wish classrooms would return to (or maintain) the monotony of simplistic rote learning (the lowest intellectual level in Bloom's taxonomy) and bottom-up grammar tasks—such as Tupper's nostalgic wish

> Simmons uses the phrase "one's language," as if all people have only one language each that they use. In fact, we all have many forms of language that we use. For example, speakers of English use informal English and formal English; technical English (based on a field of study or workplace); friendly English; evasive English; and on and on. The point is not always to be simple and accurate, as Simmons suggests; the point is to use the appropriate language for your particular purpose and for a particular audience. The more forms of English you have at your disposal, the more likely you are to be successful in your writing in any situation.

that children not be allowed to write anything until they've mastered "the laws of apostrophes, commas, and spelling." And Simmons declares, "If courses in English composition must revert to a year of chalky grammatical and syntactical drills, so be it" (2000, 49). No matter that these drills never work. (See Graham and Perin 2007.)

Another grammar rant also connects grammar with intelligence. In his title, "Clear Thinking Resides in Correct Grammar," Sonny Scott (2006) already connects "correct grammar" with "clear thinking." He is saddened by education's abandonment of sentence diagramming, saying such diagrams had a "beauty" and "logic." Like other ranters, he includes an end-of-the-world warning related to grammar: "If civilization is to continue, we must read the classics, and we must communicate our thoughts in clear and economical language." In fact, in his diatribe against an alleged "'chuck-the-grammar' movement," he skewers everything he sees wrong with society:

> In retrospect, I believe that the "chuck-the-grammar" movement was simply an extension of the "you-can-have-it-all-now" culture of the late 60's and beyond. Karaoke permitted people who couldn't play or sing to perform. Free verse let those who couldn't master meter pretend to be poets. Contemporary worship encouraged the alienated to join in the festivities without understanding either the reason for their alienation or the process of their redemption. Phys-ed classes allowed the strong who lacked the discipline to be athletes to spike the volley ball into the face of the small kids with impunity. It seems only logical that those who had no language skills be allowed to pass off their half-formed ideas in half-baked prose, I suppose. (Scott 2006)

Later on in his essay, Scott praises "Great Books," "the classics," and "unyielding traditional teachers." He hopes that "people will seek to think clearly and to communicate those thoughts in equally clear prose" (2006).

Scott calls for "clear prose," but like many ranters who plead for clarity, he never considers the possibility that what might be clear to one group of readers because of their prior knowledge and experience might not be clear to another group of equally bright readers who do not share that same background. For example, articles in physics journals might be clear to physicists but not to literary critics. Articles in literary journals might be clear to literary critics but not to physicists.

Sophisticated writers know enough to analyze the specific background knowledge of each audience for which they write, trying to gauge what will be clear to these specific readers in this specific genre and what will need to be explained to them. Good writing instructors teach their students how to do such audience analysis—which can't be done as a simple grammar drill. (They teach their students how to proofread, too, but it's not the first, last, and only thing they do.) Typical grammar ranters, however, make the simple call for "clarity," as if what *they* declare as clear or unclear will be judged exactly the same way by every other reader, in every place and time, and in every genre.

There are other problems with ranters' repeated calls for "clarity." By looking more closely at grammar rants, we discover that the emotional reaction expressed by the reader is rarely due to lack of clarity caused by the error, regardless of what the ranter says. Linguist Rei Noguchi, in *Grammar and the Teaching of Writing,* shows that readers react most strongly to errors that indicate the social status of the writer (1991, 24). In other words, the use of a class-marking *ain't,* which does not interfere with meaning at all, will annoy readers more than will a sentence with sophisticated but confusing syntax, which really does affect meaning.

Analyzing Grammar Rants About Education

Another repeating theme in many grammar rants is related to intelligence but is more focused on education, good taste, or culture—who has it and who doesn't. Many grammar ranters say or imply that those who make grammar errors lack something in manners, class, or taste and that their language choices peg them somehow as lesser people, saying things that better people would not. Yet the ranters themselves have no problem with the supreme rudeness of their own propensity to correct people, sometimes publicly, no matter the subject. In fact, the correction done publicly is a way for grammar ranters to draw attention to their own superiority. Some might say that it is the ranters who lack manners, class, and taste.

One "Dear Abby" advice column (Phillips and Phillips 2002) is an entire grammar rant with direct and indirect statements judging the education of those who make mistakes. In a long letter to her readers, Abby complains not once but twice about errors in the "between _____ and _____" construction. (See Chapter 5 for more on this.) In her second mention of this common error, she writes, "One hears *supposedly educated people* say 'between she and I' instead of the correct 'between her and me'" (Phillips and Phillips 2002, D2; our emphasis).

With her phrase "supposedly educated people," Abby implies here that those who say "between she and I" do so because of lack of education. It might be argued, however, that it is *too much* of the wrong kind of education, with its pesterings about avoiding *her* and *me* in the nominative case, that causes speakers to perform the mental high jinks that result in them blurting out "between she and I." Here's what could be happening: Educated people, so used to being harped on to avoid the "Her-and-me-went-to-the-store" error, might have learned this lesson a bit too well. They might be thinking, "Oh, I'd better not use *her* or *me*." Chances are, if left alone, most English speakers would naturally choose the correct objective pronoun following the preposition *between* ("between you and me") just by picking it up in conversation, the way they pick up other grammatical constructions. However, isolated drills and out-of-context nitpicking about "common errors" may have them overthinking these matters until they overcorrect and make an error. Linguists refer to this phenomenon as *hypercorrection*. So Abby's smug judgment about "supposedly educated people" might be more productively aimed at well-meaning but clueless grammar mavens, who may have once too often harangued dutiful schoolchildren who do take their lessons seriously and who are only trying to choose the "correct" pronoun.

The run-on sentence, or comma splice, also sparks judgments about intelligence. Peter Kalkavage, writing in *Education Digest,* says this about his pet peeve:

> No other error in writing is more instructive of the unbreakable bond that exists between writing and thinking. In the run-on sentence, the mere juxtaposition of clauses replaces the spelling out of a logical connection. A transition is implied but not expressed. *The run-on sentence is thus the very picture of intellectual hiatus.* (1998, 59; our emphasis)

Kalkavage claims, and perhaps really believes, that the comma splice confuses readers. Leaving out a coordinating conjunction (*and, but, or, nor,* etc.) is, for Kalkavage, "the very picture of intellectual hiatus" on the part of the writer. That's incredibly insulting to writers and to readers. Although even Kalkavage admits that in a comma splice the "transition is implied but not expressed," he seems to view readers as incapable of supplying this connection. What he calls "the mere juxtaposition of clauses" is an insufficient hint for the readers he apparently imagines, readers so easily confused that the lack of a coordinating conjunction completely stumps them.

We all know, including Kalkavage, perhaps, that these errors are not confusing. The lack-of-clarity trope parades as a neutral stand-in for a much more pointed critique of writers who make such errors. And whether the comma splice is an "error" at all is sometimes a function of the relative privilege of the writer who created it or the genre in which it appears. Annie

In his *English Journal* column, "Unintelligent Design: Where Does the Obsession with Correct Grammar Come From?" (May 2006), Ken Lindblom suggests that hypercorrectness may be one reason why people use the "X and I" construction where the "X and me" construction is technically correct. That is, someone might say, "The Board gave a prize to my coworker and I" instead of the standardized form: "The Board gave a prize to my coworker and me." Hypercorrectness in these cases may result from people trying very hard to avoid the "Me and X" construction that often appears in working-class English vernacular; for example, "Me and my coworker were given an award." The standardized form would be "My coworker and I were given an award." For more information, see the full column.

Proulx, the Pulitzer Prize–winning author, creates run-on sentences all the time ("Eat your bacon, don't make no trouble"; Proulx 1999, 94).

Kalkavage says later:

> One of the most annoying things one can hear from a student's lips is: "OK, it may not be what I said, but it's what I meant." The student here fails to grasp that that is precisely the task of writing—to succeed in saying what one means, *to write one's whole thought*. (1998, 59–60; our emphasis)

Kalkavage is assuming here that writing is no more than the dress of thought. He seems to believe that thoughts are formed completely in the brain prior to writing, so writing, therefore, is seen as not much more than a simple recording process. A more contemporary view of writing, however, sees it as playing a part in the actual formation of thoughts, not merely representing already-formed ideas in the brain. James Britton (1994) talks about how the acts of speaking and writing are themselves tools for generating ideas. He calls this process "shaping at the point of utterance," which describes a very different theory of writing from the one to which Kalkavage seems to subscribe.

If writing is not a mirror of the brain's workings but a tool to help the brain work, then it is counterproductive and harmful to use writing as a measure of intelligence. Instructors' opinions on who is intelligent and who is not are quite transparent to their students. So it matters what instructors believe regarding what being a grammatically correct writer means and what it does not mean. Writing *is* a tool for thinking, especially, perhaps, for English teachers and grammar ranters. But writing works better as a tool for some than it does for others. For some people, *speaking* or *drawing* works better than writing as a vehicle for generating, organizing, and processing thoughts. Composing story boards or building 3-D models are shaping tools for screen writers and engineers, while writing may actually slow down their thinking or not allow them their full range of thought. More writing teachers need to acknowledge this and design their writing pedagogies to incorporate more such tools to help all their students generate and organize ideas.

Kalkavage ends his rant with this paragraph:

> We forget that rules are also conditions of possibility. We forget, too, that grammar is a liberal as well as professional art, that it aims at the liberation of human beings. Grammar is like the magic of Prospero: It is the art of knowing how, on the one hand, to tame the Caliban of self-indulgence and, on the other, to free Ariel, free the spirit of Thought, from the cloven pine of inarticulateness. (1998, 61)

For ideas on how to employ speaking or drawing skills to help students improve as writers, see Patricia A. Dunn's *Talking, Sketching, Moving: Multiple Literacies and the Teaching of Writing* (2001).

Kalkavage comes close to anthropomorphizing grammar here ("it aims at the liberation of human beings"), and he hints at some dangerous connections between grammar and goodness. Although Kalkavage's overall purpose in his grammar rant may be to get young writers to pay more attention to grammar, his casual linkings of this issue to intelligence, and maybe even to moral goodness, are unfounded and may do more harm than good.

A sports column about baseball and grammar also includes some negative remarks about different players' choice of words, and, by implication, those players' education. Jim Nelson, in "Baseball and Correct Grammar Don't Always Mix" (2004), begins his column making fun of Dizzy Dean, who, according to Nelson, had a "propensity for destroying the King's English." Then Nelson switches to the more recent past, criticizing Texas Ranger Michael Young's comment, "We feel we have to prove ourselves. That's one thing we really thrive off of." The columnist takes issue with Young's "ending his sentence with two consecutive prepositions," helpfully suggesting instead, "thrive upon." (To us, "thrive off of" seems like a much better linguistic choice for any self-respecting baseball player than does "thrive upon.") Nelson then quotes Young's comments after a win: "We did everything we could to claw in a few runs." Here is Nelson's comment on Young's verb choice:

> "Claw in"???? There's a stat for "runs batted in" and it's common baseball phraseology to refer to "runs driven in" and "runs knocked in." If Young's "runs clawed in" can be accepted, perhaps it should more appropriately be attributed to Detroit's hitters. After all, they are the Tigers. (2004)

To be fair to Nelson, perhaps his critique of "claw in" was only to set up his line about the Tigers, which is pretty clever. But since the title of his column focuses on "correct grammar," his comments on Young's choice of verb may well be serious. It doesn't seem to occur to Nelson that Young might have wanted to avoid the conventional but humdrum phrases "runs driven in" or "runs knocked in." Young's "claw in a few runs" is a lively and vivid description; it's also, by the way, a perfectly correct grammatical choice. The runs to which Young refers weren't just "driven in"; they were tough runs, runs for which each player had to kick and scratch; they were runs "clawed in." Why is this sports columnist so comfortable criticizing that choice?

As we have seen, grammar ranters frequently use their detection of one error, or something they think is an error, to make comprehensive judgments about writers' intelligence or education. What's more, ranters seem comfortable tossing off these declarations with no evidence whatsoever, relying instead on readers' apparently shared assumptions that someone who says "between you and I" is not smart or is not educated. Why is this harmful? It's harmful because those assumptions are without basis. It's harmful because although most writers do need to learn editing and proof-reading strategies to make sure their work is professional looking, they don't need to be told, through a direct or indirect remark, that making this error means they're stupid or uneducated. Granted, novice writers should not receive patronizing pats on the head for sloppy work. Instead, they need readers to engage with their ideas, to take what they're saying seriously, to tell them what's working and what they need to work on. We writing teachers should remember that professional writers usually have spell-checkers and paid copy editors to help them clean up their manuscripts. Yes, young writers should be encouraged to be careful proofreaders, but they should not be humiliated when they miss something minor.

In the next section, following the marked-up grammar rant, are two lessons designed to help students analyze grammar rants. Doing so may help them proofread more carefully for the minor errors that cause such major fumings from grammar ranters. More importantly, these activities may help them develop close reading skills, identify inferences, and think critically about the claims and comments made by the ranters.

Marked-Up Grammar Rant

"Schools in N.Y. Give Grammar Short Shrift"

by Randi Weiner
The Journal News (October 24, 2005)

> Is he being virtuous for resisting that urge? Or is he afraid the sign makers would see such an act as not helpful but rude?

[Sam Tupper]* has a hard time resisting the urge to correct grammar, usage and spelling mistakes on signs and menus he sees around Rockland.

> This seems to be less about the error itself and more about "the people who know the difference."

He's not the only one. Writers, teachers and people who know the difference between "its" and "it's" all have stories about errors they've seen while stopped at a light, standing in line at a gas station or looking at a

> It's possible that the sign makers *do* know the difference between *its* and *it's*, but they were in a hurry and made a mistake.

> One wonders why people tell each other such stories. Does this make them feel superior?

board of lunch specials while deliberating between the hamburger or the
tuna sandwich.

Brian Monahan, deputy assistant superintendent for North Rockland schools, still remembers his conversation at a local car repair shop that had posted a "Your car serviced while your (sic) sleeping" sign a couple years ago. Yes, he eventually admitted, he was a—former—English teacher.

[Tupper] is a retired Spring Valley High School principal, but he worked 17 years as an English teacher. These days he's a motivational speaker and runs seminars on topics ranging from conflict resolution and becoming a more effective boss to team building.

One of his seminars, "Between You and I, What Happened to Good Grammar?" had been scheduled last week at a library, but was canceled because too few people signed up.

Grammar, [Tupper] said, doesn't seem to interest the average New Yorker.

He, on the other hand, has always been fascinated by it. He used to carry a camera around and take pictures of poor grammar, atrocious punctuation and egregious spelling errors as they appeared on the area's streets, stores and signs.

"The grammar out there is so poor it gets to me," he said. "It just bothers me when I hear people say certain things."

> The people who like to tell stories of other people's grammar errors seem to have more leisure time than do the busy people who make the signs or daily lunch menus.

> This man actually corrected the grammar of the person working on his car! That seems unwise.

> This seems to assume all English teachers go around correcting other people's grammar.

> The writer probably means that Monahan *is* a former English teacher.

> That's a broad generalization based on very limited evidence. Besides, maybe it was the title of Tupper's seminar, not the topic, that failed to grab people's attention.

> He seems to be more interested in the mistakes than in grammar, per se. Why the fascination with other people's mistakes?

> This supposed hypersensitivity to other people's errors is often the excuse grammar ranters use for feeling free to correct other people.

[Tupper] traces the deterioration of grammar to the 1960s, when what he called the "era of relevance" invaded the nation's schoolrooms. To try to get children connected with their subjects, the allegedly drier aspects of language were put aside, so as not to get in a child's way.

Those who had schoolchildren in the 1980s and early 1990s remember the Whole Language movement, which encouraged the youngest children to write long before they were expected to understand the laws of apostrophes, commas and spelling. The idea was that the rules would stifle a child's natural desire to write, and that a child would pick up the rules later, when he or she was older.

It's been years now since grammar was a separate subject at the middle and high school levels, and there are few, if any, people who are trained to teach it, [Tupper] said.

"You would think on the East Coast, where we pride ourselves on our educational system, that grammar would be better here," he said. "It's not. We don't teach it, so people don't learn it. It's a lost art form."

Quinton Van Wynen, director of operations at Pearl River schools, adds the Internet and computers to the list of influences that have killed grammar and spelling. He remembered trying to get his son, now 30 years old, to learn how to spell and his son asking what was the big deal now that spell-check programs took care of that.

GRAMMAR RANTS

"We don't pay attention like we used to. I blame a lot of it on the corre-spondence that goes on over the Internet," Van Wynen said. "People don't even go back and re-read and take a look and see if there were any misspell-ings. They don't even use the spell-check."

His wife, who teaches nurses, corrects their papers for facts and for gram-mar, he said, and sends papers back covered in red ink.

"She was trying to get them to be literate human beings," he said. "They looked at her as if she had two heads."

People tend to think that those who speak properly are more intelligent than those who don't, [Tupper] said. They also tend to think a properly speaking candidate is more qualified for higher-paid jobs.

Of course, there's the flip side. People who speak properly have been accused by their less grammatically correct acquaintances of being stuck up or trying to embarrass the people around them.

[Tupper] concedes he used to modify his speech when he was a teen hanging around with his friends. Now, he tells people in his seminars that they need to learn proper grammar so they can ratchet up their speech when it counts.

"Those people who can change the way they speak appropriately are people who will go places," he said.

> Is it a good use of time to rigorously proofread *all* writing? Must even informal emails be writ-ten in standardized English? If so, people will have much less time to write them.

> We hope the nurses spent enough time learning to be good nurses and that some talented nurses weren't chased out of the pro-fession by this teacher.

> Everyone here seems to assume that being a "literate human being" is only about facts and grammar.

> Being able to change one's lan-guage depending on the circum-stances is a valuable skill, and it's good that Tupper makes this point. But that's not the main message of this grammar rant. The main point seems to be that "the laws of apostrophes, com-mas and spelling" are more important than anything else regarding writing or speaking. If the assumptions Tupper, Mona-han, and Weiner seem to share are also shared by their readers, it's no wonder there is so much pressure on schools to teach such low-level skills.

> Maybe the people whose grammar Tupper is correcting are modify-ing their language for the same reason he did as a teen.

> If "people who speak properly" correct oth-ers in public, should we really feel sorry for the correctors if others find them "stuck up"?

> The "People tend to think" phrase is not in quotes, but it seems to be a paraphrase for what Tupper said. One wonders why he dis-tanced himself from that statement about intelligence rather than saying, "I think. . . ."

---

* The name "Sam Tupper" is a fictional pseudonym with which we have replaced the origi-nal name in Weiner's article.

Lesson 1

Objectives

Students will:

- define and identify commonplaces
- discuss assumptions the writer seems to take for granted that his readers will share
- think critically about the implications of those assumptions

Materials

- Handout: Questions on Grammar Rants About Intelligence

Procedures

1. Begin with a five- to ten-minute warm-up for the lesson, posing the following questions to students: Have you ever seen signs with misspellings on them? Have you heard people comment on these signs? Have you ever commented on a misspelled sign, or had your homemade signs commented upon? What assumptions do people who comment on those signs seem to make about the people who make the signs? What do you think of those assumptions or comments? Why do you think sign makers make the kinds of errors they do?

   Instructors may want students to take two minutes to think about how they'll answer this question. Students might write briefly about an incident when they saw a misspelled sign, or they might draw the sign and their reaction to it. Teachers might also show a photo of a sign with an error to start discussion. After students have gathered their thoughts, instructors can lead a large-group discussion on this for five minutes.

2. Have students work on the handout Questions on Grammar Rants About Intelligence. Students could work in pairs or groups or with the teacher in a large-group discussion at any point during class or for homework.

Handout: QUESTIONS ON GRAMMAR RANTS ABOUT INTELLIGENCE

These questions address sections of "Schools in N.Y. Give Grammar Short Shrift" by Randi Weiner.

1. Weiner writes:

   > Writers, teachers and people who know the difference between *its* and *it's* all have stories about errors they've seen while stopped at a light, standing in line at a gas station, or looking at a board of lunch specials while deliberating between the hamburger or the tuna sandwich.

   a. According to Weiner, who knows the difference between *its* and *it's*? What kinds of stories do you think these people tell? To whom? Why do you think they tell these stories? What do you think the "people who know the difference" think of the people who do not? To what extent is that a fair judgment?

   b. What kinds of signs have these *its/it's* errors? To what extent do these errors confuse readers? Under what circumstances are these lunch special signs usually written?

2. Weiner also writes: "People tend to think that those who speak properly are more intelligent than those who don't, [Tupper] said."

   a. What do you think is Tupper's idea of speaking "properly"? Who decides what it means to "speak properly"?

   b. Why does Tupper say, "People tend to think that. . . ."? Why does he not say, "I think that those who speak properly are more intelligent than those who do not"?

3. Examine this sentence by Weiner:

   > Brian Monahan, deputy assistant superintendent for North Rockland schools, still remembers his conversation at a local car repair shop that had posted a "Your car serviced while your (sic) sleeping" sign a couple years ago.

   a. We don't know much about this conversation. All we know is that a conversation took place between this former English teacher and someone at his local car repair shop. The conversation apparently focused on the use of *your* instead of *you're* on a sign at the shop. Try your hand at writing out (or simply role-playing) the conversation. How might it have started and ended?

   b. Try role-playing the conversation that took place between the former English teacher and the repair shop owner.

   c. How would you feel if you were the repair shop owner? How wise was it for the English teacher to criticize the language of the person fixing his car?

   d. What skills are valued in our society? What skills are not valued quite as much? What if the mechanic were to point out that the English teacher could not change his own oil (or whatever was being done that day)? What do you think of the English teacher's manners?

Answer Key for Handout

1a. Answers will vary, but Weiner seems very proud that she and other "writers and teachers and people who know the difference" can notice these *its/it's* errors while they're waiting for a light to change or for someone to make their hamburger. It's implied that they tell these stories to each other, drawing a distinction between those "who know the difference" and those they think do not. Perhaps telling these stories makes them feel superior to those who make the signs, which seems like an unfair judgment. It may well be that the sign makers *do* know the difference but were in a rush making the sign. Also, "knowing the difference" is not an earthshaking piece of knowledge that indicates a brilliant mind or an impressive skill level. People who run busy, successful businesses have knowledge and skills that the "people who know the difference" seem to ignore in their grammar rants.

1b. The signs under scrutiny here are probably handwritten chalkboard signs announcing lunch specials. The *its/it's* error in them is probably not confusing. The sign makers are probably dashing off these "specials" boards as part of many tasks they do as they get ready for a lunchtime rush of customers. They may not have time to proofread everything. They may not be native speakers of English. They may not be focused on language use in the same way their critics are—people who make their living working with words and language.

2a. Tupper's idea of "speaking properly" is probably similar to what typical grammar handbooks say. Although these handbooks do all agree on when to use *its* and *it's* (a fairly simple distinction), they do not always absolutely agree on other areas of grammar or usage. Who decides what is "proper"? No one. Authoritative experts like Bryan A. Garner (2009) do research and compile samples of what is written in respected publications or what is said by respected people. What is "proper" changes over time, and responsible writers of usage manuals report on that change.

2b. Tupper says, "*People* tend to think" rather than, "*I* think." He may, subconsciously, wish to distance himself a bit from this rather harsh judgment, that "those who speak properly are more intelligent than those who do not."

In *Garner's Modern American Usage* (Garner 2009)—an incredibly valuable style guide—one will find a "Language-Change Index" that shows the current stages of acceptance of different word changes in English. Garner's "Key to the Language-Change Index" includes ten humorous analogies for the different stages. For example, an "Etiquette Analogy": a word at Stage 1 (not acceptable) is like "audible farting"; Stage 2 is like "audible belching"; Stage 3 is like "overloud talking"; Stage 4 is like "elbows on the table"; and Stage 5 is "refined" (xxxv). An example of a word he believes is at Stage 1 is *ain't* "said with a straight face" (31). *Alot* as one word is at Stage 2 (37). Using the word *disenfranchise* instead of *disfranchise* is at Stage 5 (265).

3a.
and
3b.
The conversation between the English teacher and the mechanic regarding an error in the repair shop's sign might have been friendly on the surface but ultimately must have been awkward or embarrassing. Here's how we imagine the conversation:

MONAHAN: Just an oil change and an overall checkup today, Frank. I'm taking a long trip and I want to make sure everything's okay.

MECHANIC: We'll check everything out for you. You dropping off or waiting?

MONAHAN: Waiting. I'm sure it won't take long. By the way, I was just reading the sign you've got up over there.

MECHANIC: [*Busy putting Monahan's car on the lift*] Uh huh.

MONAHAN: [*Chuckling a bit*] I noticed that you have a grammatical error in it.

MECHANIC: You don't say.

MONAHAN: Yes. You wrote, "Your car serviced while *your* sleeping" Y-O-U-R, and it should be the contraction for *you are*, which is Y-O-U apostrophe R-E. You're.

MECHANIC: I'll be sure to fix that right away, as soon as I'm done with your car here.

MONAHAN: I hated to say anything, Frank, but . . .

MECHANIC: You know, this checkup may take a lot longer than I first thought.

3c. Although some people thank grammar ranters for pointing out errors in their speech or writing, we suspect that many do so through gritted teeth. It can be humiliating to have your language criticized, especially because language use, in this society, is often seen (falsely!) as a sign of a person's intelligence or education.

3d. Language skills are highly valued—especially by, as Weiner describes them, "writers and teachers and people who know the difference between 'its' and 'it's.'" So-called blue-collar skills, such as auto mechanics and plumbing, do not have the same status, though they also require intelligence, knowledge, analysis, and skill—much more so, we would argue, than forming the possessive of a pronoun. Answers will vary regarding what Monahan would think if the mechanic were to point out what Monahan obviously does not know about fixing his car.

However, that would probably not happen. Most people are not rude enough to point out what others do not know. Grammar ranters, however, seem to have no problem correcting others.

Lesson 2

Objectives

Students will:

- analyze the word choices of writers—and their critics—and make informed judgments about those word choices based on the context in which the words appear: audience, purpose, style, tone, time, place, and so on
- think critically about implied attitudes about intelligence and education, based on a speaker's language use
- speak briefly in small- or large-group class discussions
- research sports history, using library resources to access sports articles from archived newspapers, or interview witnesses
- research sticky grammar questions by consulting a variety of handbooks or reputable websites

Materials

- Handout: Questions on "Baseball and Correct Grammar Don't Always Mix" (p. 46)

Procedures

1. Begin with a five- to ten-minute warm-up for the lesson, posing the following questions to students: Have you ever heard someone correct the grammar of a public figure? Who was corrected? What did he or she say that was called into question? Who did the correcting? What do you think of these corrections? Which corrections do you think were deserved? Which ones were not deserved?

2. Have students read Jim Nelson's column, "Baseball and Correct Grammar Don't Always Mix" (2004).

3. Hand out questions on Nelson's article.

"Baseball and Correct Grammar Don't Always Mix"

by Jim Nelson
Bluefield Daily Telegraph (May 12, 2004)

Many years ago, an outcry arose from public school English teachers and some parents shortly after Hall of Fame baseball pitcher Dizzy Dean launched his broadcasting career.

Their concern didn't center upon Dean's knowledge of the game or his level of fame. They were deeply bothered that a generation of young listeners/viewers would copy Dean's propensity for destroying the King's English.

In defending his choice of phrases, Dean said, "So what if I said he slud into third or he was throwed out at second. I only made it to the second grade. If I'd been promoted to the third grade, I would have passed up my dad."

In the fifty years since Dean's electronic media debut, baseball has changed quite a bit. However, if last weekend's quotes attributed to star players are an indication, some things about the sport have remained remarkably unchanged.

Following Saturday's epic 16–15 win over Detroit, Texas Rangers' star Michael Young observed, "We feel we have to prove ourselves. That's one thing we really thrive off of." Certainly, Young set or tied some type of record by ending his sentence with two consecutive prepositions. Even more interesting, his quote prompted a question—does a team thrive "off of" something, or does it thrive "upon" something? Let history be the judge.

Rangers' second baseman Alfonso Soriano added, "That is the first time I have ever been in a game like that." Linguists may give Soriano more leeway than Young in his "my first time I" instead of "the first time I" because the Rangers' newest star is an expert at hitting the curve but is still learning the language. Young concluded his observations after the win by noting, "The bullpen did their job (should have been 'its' job), and we did everything we could to claw in a few runs." "Claw in"????. There's a stat for "runs batted in" and it's common baseball phraseology to refer to "runs driven in" and "runs knocked in." If Young's "runs clawed in" can be accepted, perhaps it should more appropriately be attributed to Detroit's hitters. After all, they are the Tigers.

From a pitching mound in his "field of dreams," Dizzy Dean must be smiling.

Handout: QUESTIONS ON "Baseball and Correct Grammar Don't Always Mix"

1. Nelson tells us that Dizzy Dean, a Hall of Fame baseball player, was made to feel he had to defend the way he spoke. Nelson says "public school English teachers" were partly responsible for the "outcry" about Dean's language. Why was the way Dizzy Dean spoke criticized? To what extent was the criticism justified? Are English teachers ever made to feel they have to defend the way they play baseball?

2. Nelson then critiques contemporary baseball players' language. Nelson has issues with Michael Young's use of two prepositions at the end of a sentence. Nelson implies that Young should have used *upon*. See below:

   "We feel we have to prove ourselves. That's one thing we really thrive off of."
   (Young's comment)

   "We feel we have to prove ourselves. That's one thing we really thrive upon."
   (Nelson's suggested change)

   Which sentence ending do you think is more appropriate for a baseball player in this context? Why?

3. Nelson goes on to criticize Texas Ranger Michael Young's speech. He focuses on this sentence by Young: "The bullpen did their job, and we did everything we could to claw in a few runs." Nelson tells us very authoritatively that "The bullpen did *their* job" should be "The bullpen did *its* job." What does your classroom grammar handbook say about collective nouns? What does the online Purdue Online Writing Lab (OWL) say about collective nouns? What do other grammar handbooks say? Could "The bullpen did *their* job" ever be correct? What do you think? If you agree that Young might be right, why does Nelson announce so surely that Young is wrong? Where does Nelson get his authority to rule on Young's pronoun choice?

4. Nelson continues to critique that same sentence from Young: "The bullpen did their job, and we did everything we could to claw in a few runs." Here's what Nelson says: "'Claw in'????? There's a stat for 'runs driven in' and 'runs knocked in.'" If Young's "runs clawed in" can be accepted, perhaps it should more appropriately be attributed to Detroit's hitters. After all, they are the Tigers. (2)

   It's possible that Nelson makes this "correction" not to critique players' language but to set up his joke about "claw" and "Tigers." But let's assume he's serious. Why do you think Young chose that verb? Do you think "runs driven in" or "runs knocked in" are better phrases here? Why or why not?

5. Read the following passage carefully. What seems to be the editing problem in it? Do you understand what he's talking about?

   Rangers' second baseman Alfonso Soriano added, "That is the first time I have ever been in a game like that." Linguists may give Soriano more leeway than Young in his "my first time I" instead of "the first time I" because the Rangers' newest star is an expert at hitting the curve but is still learning the language.

6. Why is a sports columnist writing about language use?

Answer Key for Handout

Answers to the handout's open-ended questions will vary. Here are answers we'd give:

1. Nelson says Dizzy Dean was criticized for his language use as a broadcaster because teachers felt that children would be unduly influenced by Dean's language practices. Answers will vary regarding whether or not Dean's colorful language should have been criticized and to what extent young people permanently adopt the language practices of sports figures and broadcasters. We maintain that people can differentiate among various language patterns if they aren't taught that there is only one correct way to speak in all contexts.

2. Answers will vary. However, "thrive upon," which is the grammar ranter's suggestion, seems too formal for postgame sports commentary and not suited to the context in which Young was speaking.

3. Some grammarians would agree with Nelson. The rule is that collective nouns (like *bullpen*) take a singular pronoun (like *its*) most of the time. Here's what the 2007 *Little, Brown Compact Handbook* (Aaron 2007) says:

   > Use a singular pronoun with a collective noun when referring to the group as a unit:
   >
   > > The committee voted to disband itself. (229)

   That's probably what Nelson had in mind when he says, "should have been 'its' job." But the same handbook continues:

   > When referring to the individual members of the group, use a plural pronoun:
   >
   > > The old group have gone their separate ways. (229)

   Now, if Young thought of "the bullpen" as individuals doing their separate jobs in winning the game, then he was completely justified in saying, "The bullpen did their job." After all, the entire bullpen doesn't get up at once and go out on the field, unless there's a bench-clearing brawl. Everyone knows that in baseball, individuals are called up one by one to take another individual's place in the game. So we think Young was perfectly correct using *their*.

The handbook also lists some "noncount" nouns "that take plural pronouns, including *clergy, military, police, the rich,* and *the poor*: *The police support their unions*" (229). It's not that big a leap from the handbook-approved "The police support their unions," to the sentence Nelson critiqued: "The bullpen did their job." Young's use of *their* in that sentence is at the very least arguably correct.

4. Answers will vary. However, "claw in" is grammatically correct, if perhaps a bit too creative for some listeners. "Claw in" is much more vivid than "runs driven in" or "runs knocked in." We like it.

5. It looks like a copy editor might have accidentally "corrected" the very sentence Nelson is criticizing Soriano for getting wrong, which makes the passage very confusing. If this is the case, then Nelson and the copy editor missed *their* error in fixing Soriano's error, which, if left alone, might have made this section of Nelson's paragraph comprehensible. Nelson criticizes Soriano, who was speaking off the cuff after an exciting game. Nelson and his copy editor are paid to create error-free prose, and yet they missed this confusion-causing mistake in this grammar rant. We don't mean to make such a fuss about Nelson's error, but he started it!

6. Answers will vary.

Follow-Up Research and Writing Projects

1. Have students research the "outcry" from parents and teachers regarding Hall of Famer Dizzy Dean's speech. Who was Dizzy Dean? When did he play and what is he famous for? What *was* his broadcasting career? What are some of his famous quotes? What *did* parents and teachers say about his speech? Did others defend his speech? This would be a good time for students to learn how to access newspaper archives. It would also be a good time for them to learn interviewing skills. Their oldest relatives might have vivid memories of Dizzy Dean's baseball accomplishments, his broadcasts, or what others said about him.

2. Have students investigate what various grammar handbooks or online grammar websites (the Purdue OWL is a good one) say about collective nouns and the pronouns that should be used with them. Is it always the case that a collective noun like *bullpen* takes a singular pronoun? What

are some exceptions and examples? To what extent is it crystal clear whether Young or Nelson chose the "correct" pronoun in "The bullpen did ____ job"? Students could also research what these various handbooks or online grammar websites say about ending a sentence with a preposition. (For examples of rules on which handbooks disagree, see Chapter 5.)

3. Have students read the sports pages in their local newspaper, in a magazine, or at an online sports website. Have them examine the quotations from players who are cited. How do the people quoted use language? Which quotes are vivid? Which quotes have "errors"? Should players speak "correct" English? Who gets to say what that is?

Bryan A. Garner says the rule that claims English sentences should never end in a preposition "is a remnant of Latin." He also says Winston Churchill's famous quip in response to someone criticizing this habit in his speech should be the last word on the matter: "That is the type of arrant pedantry up with which I will not put" (Garner 2009, 564).

3

Grammar Rants on Spelling

Background Information

We include spelling in a book about grammar rants because spelling frequently shows up in a string of complaints about other people's writing and because complaints about spelling usually devolve into a general complaint that lumps spelling, usage, and real issues of grammar into one general category. We also focus on spelling here because spelling, like grammar, is frequently cited by ranters as an indication regarding a user's intelligence or morality: some people think good spelling equals a smart, moral person; some people think bad spelling equals a not-so-smart, immoral person.

Contrary to popular opinion, spelling ability is an indication of neither intelligence nor morality. Although mistakes in spelling can drive readers to distraction, spelling ability is not related to writing ability. Good spellers can be bad writers; bad spellers can be good writers. As rhetoric scholars Crowley and Hawhee point out:

> People have trouble spelling English words because English spelling is irregular and erratic; it is irregular and erratic because it reflects accidents of linguistic history. For example, the "gh" in words like *light* and *bright* is there because it used to be pronounced. (2009, 413)

For some reason, however, the general public is fascinated by spelling—or journalists think they are. News about spelling bees frequently appears on page 1 of local and national newspapers. The winners of these bees get their pictures in the paper, receive impressive prizes (totaling $40,000 for the 2010 winner), and appear on television. In fact, in recent years, ESPN has begun covering the National Spelling Bee like a sports competition.

It's ironic that this fascination with people being able to spell continues unabated in an age when, except for spelling bees, there are few occasions for people to have to spell something off the top of their head, without help. In a few professions, of course, some documents are still handwritten, and some teachers still write on old-fashioned blackboards. Yes, spelling is still important. But spell-checkers on word processors are now fairly sophisticated, if not infallible, and voice-to-text programs, even with their glitches, eliminate many spelling problems. (This is nothing new to professionals or the wealthy, who have secretaries who capture their oral compositions in correctly spelled and edited text.) To judge by what appears in front-page news stories, however, people are fascinated not with spell-checkers or voice/speech recognition programs (as impressive as these programs are), but with children up on a stage dictating one painful letter after another of an obscure, multisyllabic word.

Even high-level teacher-leaders can be consumed by concerns about correct spelling. Several years ago, Richard Mills, then New York State Commissioner of Education, wrote a column in which he described a visit he made to an elementary school. When a first-grade student brought him several pages of a short story draft he had written, the first thing Commissioner Mills did was point out a spelling error in the six-year-old child's draft (Mills 2004, 10). What makes even some educational leaders focus like lasers on spelling errors even with very young children (even in the face of an accomplishment such as writing a several-page story)? Some answers may be found in how teachers have been trained for over a hundred years.

One of us (Ken Lindblom) authored a column for NCTE's *English Journal* in 2006, entitled "Unintelligent Design: Where Does the Obsession with Correct Grammar Come From?" (2006) in which he outlined problematic attitudes about spelling among faculty at a very influential teacher training institution in the mid-nineteenth century. Illinois State Normal University was so concerned with the spelling of its students that they were required to take a twenty-five-word spelling test every morning until they could go a full term without misspelling more than one word. And, even if the students

Spelling correctly is a relatively new idea. Standardized spelling as a concept didn't exist before the eighteenth century, when scholars first decided that it would be a good idea for everyone to spell words the same way. Before that, writers would compose words and readers were simply expected to be able to decipher them.

passed this requirement, if a professor ever found a misspelling in a student's writing (even if that student correctly edited the spelling before turning the paper in), the student was required to take the spelling tests again for another term. The professor who ran these exams made his position on the matter very clear when he said that a good teacher "will leave no means untried to correct [this] *almost universal evil*" (Stetson 1867, 113; italics added here and throughout this paragraph). Stetson was not the only faculty member at ISNU to connect correct spelling with good morals. Another professor once said that students left the university with a "fonetic consciousness and a *fonetic conscience*" (De Garmo qtd. in Harper 1935, 86). Referencing spelling, then ISNU President Richard Edwards wrote, "The Normal University considers it a worthy service to do all that is possible to remedy this *evil*" (qtd. in Harmon 1995, 89). In 1874, the State of Illinois Board of Education issued a statement of support of the faculty beliefs at ISNU that "agreed with the professors that laxness in such matters as spelling betrayed a *weakness in character* or a *moral lapse*" (Harper 1935, 109).

These moralistic attitudes about spelling had a dramatic effect on the students' beliefs at ISNU (all of whom were training to be teachers). One student, decades after graduating from ISNU, said he still believed that "if a word is spelled in two ways [he] always [chose] the harder, because it afforded more mental discipline in the learning of it" (Felmley 1915, 22).

Even today, spelling fascinates journalists, who often link it with intelligence or morality. As we scoured newspapers and blogs for this book, we found articles on crime that focus not on the crime itself but on spelling, for example, in a bank stickup note. Such articles often include snide remarks linking the bad spelling or grammar with the crime, as if there's a mutual understanding between reporters and readers that of course those bad spellers are going to end up as bank robbers—and that those bad bank robbers are inevitably bad spellers. As we will explain, reporters depend on this assumption and foreground it in their stories, even when police tell them that the bank robbers are deliberately disguising their usual writing style in order to throw off police.

This insistence on the part of journalists to make fun of real or deliberate spelling errors made by criminals might be an amusing pattern to notice, except for the unspoken message it gives to law-abiding citizens for whom spelling is not what Diana Jean Schemo calls a "virtue" (2004, 2). The unspoken message is that bad spelling is a sign of immoral behavior. Chrissy Ijams, who seems to revel in her intolerance for deliberately misspelled advertisements (Kwik Mart, Tastykake, etc.), has this to say about her insistence on

The Simplified Spelling Society was organized over 100 years ago to advocate for easier ways of spelling English words; for example, "bred" for *bread*, "paragraf" for *paragraph*, "alternativ" for *alternative*, and "dispeld" for *dispelled*. Sounds like an extremist movement by a bunch of out-there radicals, right? Here were some of the members of the Simplified Spelling Society's board in 1909: Andrew Carnegie, Samuel L. Clemens (Mark Twain), Melvil Dewey (inventor of the Dewey Decimal System), Isaac K. Funk (of Funk and Wagnall's Dictionary), Henry Holt (publisher), William James (Harvard professor), and U.S. President Theodore Roosevelt. The organization remains active today as The Spelling Society (www.spellingsociety.org/).

correct spelling: "I have always had a strong sense of right and wrong" (2004). Somehow, in many of these stories, views regarding correct and incorrect spelling slide too easily into "right" and "wrong" in the moral sense.

Some readers may think that we are against good spelling (we're not), or in favor of bad spelling (we're not), or in favor of lowering standards on spelling accuracy (we're not). We know all too well that some readers make instant, lasting judgments about writers based on how they spell. We ourselves appreciate a well-edited, carefully spell-checked piece of writing. Therefore, we encourage instructors to continue to teach their students to proofread and edit their final drafts attentively.

That said, there are other, much higher standards to which students should be held. Good spelling requires memorization or access to a good spell-check program. However, if students are to develop as writers, they need instruction and practice in reading increasingly sophisticated texts and being exposed to a variety of genres; they need practice in generating ideas for their writing project and anticipating readers' needs; they need to work on developing and organizing their ideas, and they need to work on style. Harsh critics of a misspelled word may simply be trying to get people to pay more attention to something they think is important. But harping too much on a low-level skill like spelling may distract writers from more important skills.

Also, these extreme reactions to misspellings might have negative unintended consequences: If young writers are made to feel lazy or stupid because of what the general public seems to think about people who make spelling errors, those who have trouble spelling may decide to protect themselves by simply not exposing their writing to those who are too ready to pounce on errors. Instead of working even harder to memorize spelling words that seem to come so easily to some people, some students may avoid writing or avoid school altogether. At the very least, they will write as little as possible in school and out. For an in-depth example of this problem, see Lindblom, Banks, and Quay (2007), who write about Abbie Reynolds, a mid-nineteenth-century graduate of Illinois State Normal University whose self-confidence as a writer was deeply eroded as a result of faculty attitudes about grammar, spelling, and learning in general.

We intend our analysis of media coverage of stories about spelling to get instructors thinking about how to balance what they think is important. The lessons at the end of the chapter are meant to get students thinking critically about what it means to be a good writer, and what it means—and doesn't mean—to be a good or bad speller.

Analyzing News Stories About Spelling Bees

By examining newspaper articles covering spelling bees, we can discover society's shared assumptions about spellers, in the same way analyzing grammar rants reveals hidden assumptions about writers. We see, though, that most stories are not really about the winner. They are about the losers. We're given far more details about which children lost, when, and what they did wrong, than we're given about the winner or about the overall purpose of spelling bees.

On the front page of the local section of the June 4, 2010 *Times Union* (Albany, NY), in a story about spelling bees, the headline, abstract, and lead all tell the story of a young contestant's failure. The verbs used in each sentence stress not the honor of making it to the national competition, but the child's loss. In the headline, "Spelling Bee Claims at Least One from Area," it is the spelling bee that is personified, the spelling bee that is the agent of the action. The verb *claims*—usually reserved for disasters in which people die (as in "Hurricane Claims Thousands of Lives," or "Plane Crash Claims Three Victims")—here seems overblown. The abstract under the headline says that the local girl "fails" to reach the next level. And the lead says for the third time that she "won't move on." We find out in the second paragraph that the eighth-grader participated in the "prestigious" bee in Washington, D.C., because she had won a regional contest. It is her loss, however, which is the focus of this story. We're told about that loss for the fourth time at the end of the second paragraph, when it's said that the girl "stumbled" in a later round of the tournament, "misspelling the word 'caballero', which is a Spanish horseman" (2010, D1).

The word this fourteen-year-old "stumbled" on was obscure enough for the writer to define it for the paper's adult readers, with no hint of the irony involved (that the word is so little used—or needed—that it must be defined for the audience). The news of this piece, after all, is the child's error, not her accomplishments. In fact, so eager is the paper to bring us the news of her loss that the writer and the paid copy editor both miss what most American handbooks would call a comma error in the phrase above (most say the comma after *caballero* should be inside the quotation mark).

Spelling bees are TV reality shows about children. People want to know—want to be voyeurs watching—the exact moment when the speller gets the word *wrong.* They want to witness the look on the child's face, the humiliation, the turning and walking off the stage, just like the adult losers leave the

---

ESPN now airs National Spelling Bees as it does wrestling, golf, baseball, or other sports events. It may be good that spelling is treated like athletic skill. After all, although the physical talents and mental concentration of gifted athletes are admirable and entertaining, they don't—in and of themselves—produce anything of value. Memorizing obscure words and being able to reproduce them on command in a high-pressure situation is more like making a good putt or throwing a good pitch than it is like being an especially intelligent person.

stage of *Project Runway* or roll their suitcases to a waiting cab on *The Apprentice*. This is the dramatic point at which they are "wrong," "fired," or "out."

Another newspaper, *The Pantagraph* (Bloomington/Normal, IL), also stresses the failure of a local child. A headline about a spelling bee reads: "Lincoln Speller's Run Ends in Round 3" (Loda 2002). On that same day, May 31, 2002, this piece of news shared space on the front page with these three news stories: (1) seven priests being removed by the Peoria diocese because of sexual abuse allegations; (2) then-Governor George Ryan's failed state budget and a critical, upcoming midnight deadline; (3) a formal ceremony in New York City to mark the end of the painful World Trade Center cleanup. Rounding out the front page was the coverage of a young girl's defeat in the spelling bee.

Not only was the young girl's failure at the national bee announced in the headline; her failure is repeated in the lead: "Another word for mouthwash ended Alison [name deleted]'s run Thursday. . . ." (The other word for mouthwash is *collutorium*, which she missed by one letter.) This story might have started with the fact that Alison was one of only 250 students from across the nation to go to Washington for this contest, or that she was only one of ninety remaining by the beginning of round 3, or that she had won the local spelling bee, sponsored by that very newspaper. But this story begins with what she did wrong and ends with a mistake made by last year's local representative to the national contest. (The next day, the paper did have a brief editorial on page 14 congratulating Alison for winning the local contest.)

In another report on the Scripps National Spelling Bee in Washington, this one in 2007, *The Villages Daily Sun* has this headline: "California Teen Wins Bee with 'Serrefine'" (White 2007). Despite the laudatory headline on the front page, however, this article, too, is mostly about losing. We're told that the first runner-up, the Canadian Nate [name deleted], "flubbed the medical word 'coryza' by adding the letter 'h.'" This sentence, with its verb *flubbed*, seems to imply not only that everyone knows what *coryza* means but that only a fool would add the letter *h* to it. The news writer seems almost gleeful about Nate's "flub," as if he had it coming:

> Until then, Nate had been quite the showman, waving celebrity-like to the audience after each word and basking in the cheers from a row that waved red-and-white maple leaf flags. (White 2007, A6)

The writer seems to disapprove of Nate's enjoyment of his successful spellings, his pride in representing Canada, and his appreciation of the cheers of

The Tony Award–winning Broadway play, *The 25th Annual Putnam County Spelling Bee*, offers an amusing look at spelling bee culture. Before the play begins, several audience members are recruited to participate in a mock spelling bee on stage (www.spellingbeethemusical.com/).

his countrymen. We're asked to compare the teenager who made it this far to an overly proud celebrity, foolishly enjoying what will be his swan song. There's a hint of "he-had-it-coming-ness," almost like the just punishment of someone committing the sin of pride.

The last eight or so paragraphs of this article continue with the litany of failure:

> The field was narrowed to 15 finalists, but eight were gone after the initial round, and two more faltered in the next round . . .

> Joseph faltered on "aniseikonia" (a visual defect), while Prateek missed "oberek" (a Polish folk dance) and Isabel was out on "cyanophycean" (a kind of algae).

> Several of the top favorites were eliminated early in the finals . . .

> Jonathan [name deleted], 14, of Gilbert, Ariz., who stumbled on "girolle" (a kind of mushroom) . . .

> Matthew [name deleted], 12, of Albuquerque, N.M., couldn't handle "fauchard" (a long-handled weapon) . . .

> Perennial favorite Samir [name deleted] was eliminated . . .

> He ended his bee career with a tie for 34th.

> Samir wiped away tears as he talked about his gaffe.

Again, most of the words these children "stumbled on" or "couldn't handle" are so obscure that they need to be explained. Words used in the 2004 Scripps contest, for example, included *triskaidekaphobia, acesodyne, rijsttafel,* and *epixylous* (Associated Press 2004). We're rarely told about the tough words these children *did* spell correctly that landed them in the final round.

What can it mean that spelling bees are covered so thoroughly, that reports about them land on the front page next to stories about the tragedy at the World Trade Center? Is it that the schoolchild in each of us enjoys watching "the smart kids" fail? It may be our fascination with the grueling preparation of the spellers or our admiration for their single-minded dedication, although that's rarely reported. It may involve the high drama of the competition, but in sports the reports generally focus on how the winners won, not how the losers lost. In sports, the number of points gained by any legal methods in the game is covered; in a spelling bee, only the absence of error counts. The second an error happens, it's over for the child. Or is it our obsession for "correctness," even for words we've never heard of? It may be that how to spell a word is one of the few skills with a clear, published, right or wrong answer, and we appreciate the clarity and logic of a simple question with a simple answer. It can simply be looked up in a dictionary, such as the one designated for the Scripps National Spelling Bees: *Webster's Third New International Dictionary*.

Columnist Cal Thomas links being able to spell well with a higher-order knowledge. After he tells us that "the top three finishers" in the 2000 Spelling Bee were homeschooled, he implicitly links spelling skills with "real knowledge" and "wisdom":

> Contrast the pursuit of excellent and unique personal attention that are the norm among home schoolers with what occurs in government schools, where the curriculum is often dumbed-down and non-academic subjects take time away from acquiring real knowledge and the endangered species known as wisdom. (2000, 1)

Although his column is mostly an argument for homeschooling and a critique of public schools, his focus on homeschooled children winning or placing in spelling and geography bees highlights what he considers important for children to learn. He doesn't say so outright, but his introduction about spelling bees is followed immediately with a remark about "the pursuit of excellence" and "real knowledge" and "the endangered species known as wisdom." That's a big leap: from spelling correctly to "the endangered species known as wisdom," and Thomas says little to support this connection.

Because Thomas does not actually make an argument or provide evidence that spelling skills equal wisdom, he seems to assume that his readers will go along with him. He might be surprised, however, on one expert's opinion on this subject. Evan O'Dorney, the thirteen-year-old who won the 2007 Scripps National Spelling Bee, had this to say about the kind of knowledge involved in his win: "The spelling is just a bunch of memorization" (White 2007, A6). Now there's an excellent speller who *also* has strong critical thinking skills!

What do spelling bees, media coverage of them, and assumptions made about the skills involved in spelling correctly have to do with writing instruction? Many of the comments and implied arguments made about good spellers and correct spelling rely on commonplaces, shared assumptions between writers and readers. Because they are unarticulated assumptions, they are rarely examined for their accuracy.

If student writers have a few spelling errors in their essays for school, sometimes the same assumptions are at play in comments instructors make to these students and judgments students might make (falsely) about themselves. If we all believe that spelling correctly indicates a superior form of "real knowledge" or "wisdom," or that it is a sign of some kind of moral superiority, there's a danger that minor spelling errors might be seen as a lack of wisdom or a lapse in morals in writers who make spelling errors. Because these are fairly harsh judgments about people's intelligence and moral standing, many writers whose spelling is poor might choose not to show much of their writing to their teachers, thus avoiding explicit or implicit insults. They might limit their school writing to a few sentences or "undeveloped" paragraphs. They might not hand in their writing. They might drop out. This is obviously a tragedy for the individual, but it's also a tragedy for the rest of the world. How many otherwise talented people have left school too dispirited to rise to their full potential because they are poor spellers?

Without question, everyone should attempt to hand in clean, correct copy. And teachers writing on blackboards need to be extra careful about their spelling. Spelling is important—so important, in fact—that writers and their instructors need to keep in mind that spelling skills (good or bad) can trigger in readers some strong, knee-jerk judgments about those writers.

While those hasty and false judgments are not going to disappear any time soon, writers might benefit from knowing that although good spelling demands a certain kind of exacting, word-based talent and a single-minded dedication, it is also the result of ultimately low-level memorization skills. One way to help writers both pay attention to their spelling and have a more reasonable attitude about what it means to be a good or bad speller is to have them analyze news stories about spelling bees. These are easy to find. Just check the front page of local or national newspapers in early June every year, when the Scripps National Spelling Bee comes around again.

Analyzing News Stories About Spelling, Grammar, and Crime

The common assumptions that spelling bee reporters seem to depend on their readers to share have a parallel in other published stories about spelling. What we saw in Chapter 1, insinuations linking bad grammar with moral flaws, are similar to winking remarks made by writers reporting on crimes in which writing or spelling plays a role. Society seems to expect bad grammar or poor spelling from certain people, especially those who are morally suspect. Sometimes journalists writing news stories about criminals delight in the errors criminals produce, making the incorrect grammar or spelling, rather than the larger crime, the angle.

In a story about a bank robber dubbed the "Spelling Bee Bandit" because of the misspellings that appeared in the stickup notes he wrote in a two-year bank robbing career in Long Island, New York, the headline reads, "Police: Misspellings Were Just a Ploy" (Vargas 2005). After giving examples of such misspellings (*robri* and *kwik*), the rest of the short article focuses on puzzlings about how the now forty-three-year-old culprit could turn out to be a bank robber when he never missed school as a child and his grades "were a steady stream of A's and B's." The police and the reporter seem to marvel that the robber used the ill-gotten loot to pay his bills and his mortgage. Everyone seems to wonder how such a "good kid," good speller, and regular, mortgage-paying citizen could end up as a bank robber—a profession, they seem to imply, reserved for the bad spellers, school skippers, and those who don't pay mortgages. Even the robber himself used these assumptions in his method of operation, deliberately spelling poorly in his notes to confuse authorities on "the type of person" they were looking for. Playing on these widely held assumptions served the robber well, as he avoided detection during two years of successful bank robbing.

In a story about a high school girl arrested for robbing a bank, *Pittsburgh Tribune-Review* columnist Eric Heyl (2003) makes the holdup note the focus of his essay.* His column is meant to be amusing, and Heyl seems to relish the wordplay this story about grammar, spelling, and bank robbing seems to provide. The headline, "It's a Crime Grammar Means Little to Robber," is the first of such connections. Then he talks about the grammar and usage errors the robber "committed." He says later that she "should be sentenced to mandatory composition classes" and that she "is guilty of assaulting the English language, and now she must pay the price."

In his scrutiny of the holdup note, Heyl says it is "atrociously constructed," and that "concocting something as bad as the following isn't a good sign one has the ability to elude police" (2003, 1). Then he prints the holdup note for us to see:

> Put all the money in the bag that you could without making any noise or sudden movement that could cause you your life and your family's. Don't even think about putting any dye or anything that don't belong or I will see to it that you never make it home, so don't (expletive) with me.

---

* We thank Val Perry for bringing this story to our attention.

Heyl begins by making a crack about what he thinks are run-on sentences. (They're not.) Near the end of his essay, he himself creates a sentence fragment—though it's probably deliberate. (Published columnists have a poetic license denied, apparently, to bank robbers.)

He also criticizes her for not saying where, exactly, to not put the dye (as if the teller would be wondering about this) and for not saying "where not to add any inappropriate item" (as if the teller would be confused about this, too). Right after he slams her writing for not being detailed enough, Heyl reports that the FBI said the note stuck out to them because it was so much longer than others of its kind. Apparently fewer details are better in the "genre" of stickup notes.

The next several paragraphs focus on general comments FBI spokesperson Jeff Killeen had about holdup notes, grammar, and education:

> But grammar and usage errors such as the ones [this bank robber] committed can be found in even the briefest holdup note, according to Killeen.
> "Not everyone who robs a bank has a bachelor's degree in English," he explained. "We don't see many bank robbers with post-high school educations. Maybe if they had them, they wouldn't be robbing banks." (Heyl 2003, 2)

In a previous paragraph, Killeen had just said that most holdup notes "give very succinct instructions to the teller, like, 'Your money or else'" (Heyl 2003, 2). Grammar and usage problems in these notes were not mentioned as something that tellers had trouble deciphering. And the implied link with lack of education and crime could use some context: According to 2007 U.S. census data, only about 27.5 percent of adults complete a bachelor's degree, so it should not be surprising that any random person, including a bank robber, does not hold a college degree. And the robber who is the subject of Heyl's article was still in high school. It's probably true that certain kinds of crime are more often committed by those who do not finish high school. (And aren't white collar crimes like bank fraud committed by people who *do* hold certain kinds of college degrees?) But the casual linking of bad grammar or misspellings, lack of education, and criminal behavior taps into the same assumptions we've seen (in Chapters 1 and 2) linking bad grammar with bad morals or lack of education.

Are we reading too much into a columnist's reading too much into a bank robber's holdup note? After all, he seems to have intended his essay as a lighthearted commentary on a stickup note that had some errors in it. What's the harm?

First of all, the situation can't have been amusing for the teller whose life was threatened or for the teenager whose life was probably ruined by her decision to rob this bank. It was an interesting decision the columnist made: to compose a humor piece about a bank robbery that so seriously affected the lives of at least two people and to trivialize the event by focusing on grammar errors in the holdup note, and then make insinuations about her not having a college degree. The columnist is probably a college graduate who has a copy editor paid to proofread his work. The government spokesperson no doubt is also college educated. But what message do readers who are not college educated or who have occasional problems with their spelling or grammar get? They get to see themselves linked, through insinuation and unstated assumptions, to incompetent criminals.

These examples linking bad spelling with moral corruption are not rare. A 2004 Long Island *Newsday* story (Bonilla 2004) had the following headline: "This 'Rober' Means 'Bizness'" with the subheading, "Police seek 'Spelling Bee Dropout' linked to 7 crimes." This news story begins by focusing on the notes the culprit hands to tellers, notes described as being filled with grammar and spelling errors. Even though it's reported in the same story that police believe the robber is deliberately disguising both his appearance and his handwriting, opening the possibility or probability that the inconsistent misspellings are also deliberate, Bonilla continues to pursue the criminal-as-dunce angle, comparing this robber to a character in an old Woody Allen movie (*Take the Money and Run*), an incompetent bank robber with spelling problems.

Bonilla tells us that the robber "can't even spell 'robbery,'" telling the bank employees that it is a "robery" or a "robrey." Even after the fact is mentioned in the story that "police think this guy may not be as much of a dunce as he appears" and that, according to police Detective Vincent O'Leary, "It's possible that he's pretty smart," the reporter tells us later in the story that the robber "even managed to spell 'robbery' correctly." If the robber is indeed trying to throw police off the track, and the journalist has just reported this clever plan, why the continued amazement that the robber can spell? The use of *even* here shows this journalist's determination to link the criminal with incompetent spelling, despite the police detective's apparent view that the bad spelling is a deliberate ruse.

In a similar way, another news story about a criminal focuses on grammar mistakes. This journalist, too, seems determined to link immoral actions with bad grammar. In a short Associated Press news story at CNN.com, we are told about a prisoner who arranged for his own release by having a fax

In Woody Allen's *Take the Money and Run*, a would-be bank robber gets caught when a teller can't read his handwritten stickup note. The teller enlists a dozen other bank employees in trying to determine if the robber has a "gub" or a "gun."

sent to the prison demanding he be freed. In this piece (Associated Press 2007), we're told by whomever filed the story that the fax "contained grammatical errors, was not typed on letterhead and was faxed from a local grocery store."

The AP writer seems to assume that the grammar errors alone should have made it obvious to authorities that the fax was from a prisoner. Further, he or she seems to assume readers will also view prisoners as people who use bad grammar. The officials referred to in the article, however, were more alarmed that they did not notice the fax came from a grocery store, pointing out that it was not routine to examine the origin of such a fax. Although the AP writer insinuated that the errors should have tipped everyone off, Greg Taylor, one of the officials quoted, pointed out that "misspellings on orders are common."

In both cases, it is the journalists, not the police, who force a connection between criminal behavior and bad spelling or grammar. Even when told otherwise and even after reporting they've been told otherwise (that the bad spelling on the stickup notes is a deliberate fake-out or that bad spelling on legitimate orders is not unusual), these journalists insisted on focusing their stories on the bad grammar or spelling of criminals.

Are all these linkings just harmless fun? The lessons in the next section—following the marked-up grammar rant—are designed to help students read for details and draw inferences from columns and news stories about spelling. Some lessons could also be used to teach or review genre conventions. Most importantly, these lessons should help students develop critical thinking skills, helping them locate, name, and possibly question harmful assumptions and insinuations circulating, unquestioned, in our society.

Marked-Up Grammar Rant

"It's a Crime Grammar Means Little to Robber"

by Eric Heyl

Pittsburgh Tribune-Review (January 18, 2003)

Capable bank robbers seldom flub the holdup note. Like Olympic skaters who execute the challenging triple lutz, the successful bank robber does not botch that part of the presentation.

> In the first three paragraphs, the article leads us to believe that the holdup note is the reason the robber is not successful. Later, we find out that the note is not the reason she was caught.

Jamie [name deleted] is not a successful bank robber.

The 18-year-old Peabody High School senior proved this Wednesday when she was charged with robbing the PNC Bank at Fifth Avenue Place, Downtown. She subsequently confessed to the crime.

The holdup note itself didn't lead to [her] apprehension. Police found one of her fingerprints at the crime scene.

But had you seen the message before [the robber] presented it to the teller, you likely and accurately would have concluded she was destined for arrest. Concocting something as bad as the following isn't a good sign one has the ability to elude police:

> People who are eighteen are, of course, considered adults. This bank robber, though, is a high school student in the local community. It might be argued that what she's done to her life is tragic, not humorous.

> "Put all the money in the bag that you could without making any noise or sudden movement that could cause you your life and your family's. Don't even think about putting any dye or anything that don't belong or I will see to it that you never make it home, so don't (expletive) with me."

Even in Pittsburgh, where the word "slippy" often is used to describe winter street conditions, most people probably would find [the] note atrociously constructed.

> This paragraph implies that people who make mistakes in writing or spelling are stupid. It even implies that bad writers in general are "destined for arrest."

> The spelling and grammar of this note seem to us to be the least remarkable things about it.

> The writer calls her note "bad" and "atrociously constructed." Her errors include *could* instead of *can*, and *cause* instead of *cost*. She also says "don't belong" instead of "doesn't belong." Finally, she should probably have a comma after *belong*, because it is a compound sentence.

There are no run-on sentences in the note. There may be sentences that the columnist thinks are too long. The second sentence could use a comma after *belong*, but the independent clauses are linked, legitimately, with co-coordinating conjunctions. Why is Heyl finding errors that don't actually exist in this note?

It's common knowledge where not to put the dye. In this paragraph, the columnist seems to be really stretching to support his allegation that the note is "atrociously constructed."

Obviously, the robber is referring to a dye pack, a GPS tracker, or anything else that could cause the robber to be caught. The teller would know this from the note, but Heyl is being deliberately dense about it to make his point that the robber's note is poorly written.

Ignore the run-on sentences if you can, but how do you ignore "*cause* you your life"? Similarly poor word choices found in high school English essays have been known to cost students passing grades.

The note orders the teller not to "put any dye," but it neglects to detail where not to put it. Likewise, while the teller was instructed not to "add anything that don't belong" (like what, a snow tire?), no specific mention is made of where not to add any inappropriate item.

There was one small plus for the poor teller who had to wade through this mess before forking over nearly $1,000 to [the robber]. The expletive was correctly spelled.

The length of [the robber's] holdup demand stands out from similar communiques. "They usually give very succinct instructions to the teller, like, 'Your money or else,'" said Jeff Killeen, a spokesman for the FBI's Pittsburgh office.

But grammar and usage errors such as the ones [the robber] committed can be found in even the briefest holdup note, according to Killeen.

"Not everyone who robs a bank has a bachelor's degree in English," he explained. "We don't see many bank robbers with post-high school educations. Maybe if they had them, they wouldn't be robbing banks."

George Fisher owns the Penn Aiken Dairy in Garfield, where [the robber] once worked. He gives the impression that [she] has the potential to craft significantly better holdup demands.

Killeen's comment plays to widely held assumptions. But since most American citizens do *not* have a "bachelor's degree in English," it's not all that surprising that most bank robbers are not English majors. What college degrees do those who commit white-collar crimes hold? What college degrees are useful to those who commit bank fraud or Ponzi schemes? Those questions are not discussed here.

The columnist is having fun with words in this humor column. Note *crime* in the title and *committed* here.

"She speaks very well. She's a little more clever than people give her credit for," Fisher said. Not quite clever enough to avoid her arrest last year for stealing more than $3,000 from the dairy, you understand, but still pretty clever.

It's nice Fisher speaks so highly of his larcenous ex-employee, but [the robber's] writing skills obviously need work. In addition to any criminal penalty she receives for robbing the bank, [she] should be sentenced to mandatory composition classes until she can consistently construct a grammatically correct holdup note.

She is guilty of assaulting the English language, and now she must pay the price. As [she] might put it, it's a classic example of cost and affect.

For someone who is quick to point out the bank robber's "run-ons," which were not run-ons, Heyl has no problem writing a sentence fragment. It's no doubt a deliberate fragment, but someone who nit-picks someone else's writing might want to be more careful. This fragment must have been okay with the columnist's paid copy editor, too.

Now, as a joke, Heyl attributes mistakes to the robber that she never even made.

The columnist has more fun with crime-related words applied to grammar trivia.

More fun with crime words and grammar: "guilty," "assaulting," and "now she must pay the price."

Here is an example of anthropomorphism, in which writers treat language as if it is a living creature, able to be victimized ("assaulted"). Grammar ranters frequently use this rhetorical move to make language seem like the victim of bad people.

This essay is meant as a humor piece. Bank robbers are probably fair game for columnists, but this crime has ruined the life of a high school girl, and the episode was surely not humorous to the bank teller, whose life was threatened. Shared assumptions between writer and readers drive this piece. These shared assumptions—about who is smart or stupid and who is moral or immoral—might be quite harmful to law-abiding citizens who spell a word wrong now and then or use one word when they mean to use another. And it's really not funny.

Lesson 1

Objectives

Students will:

- read sentences closely, examining them for usage, spelling, and punctuation problems
- investigate what different grammar handbooks or online sites say about what constitutes a run-on and a fragment
- develop inference skills by thinking critically about the explicit and implicit judgments a columnist makes about someone else's writing style and apparent intelligence
- think critically about the columnist's choice of topic and what it suggests about our society

Materials

- Internet access
- Handout: Worksheet on "It's a Crime Grammar Means Little to Robber" (p. 69)
- Several different grammar handbooks for the classroom and/or access to the Purdue Online Writing Lab (Google Purdue OWL), Grammar Girl's Quick and Dirty Tricks (http://grammar.quickanddirtytips.com/), or other reliable source for grammar, usage, and punctuation

Procedures

1. Begin with this warm-up: Watch the first minute and a half of a YouTube clip (bank robber scene in which tellers can't read spelling in Virgil Stockwell's holdup note) of the Woody Allen film, *Take the Money and Run* (www.youtube.com/watch?v=-UHOgkDbVqc).

2. Have students read "It's a Crime Grammar Means Little to Robber."

3. Have students reread the bank robber's note, as well as the several short paragraphs following that note, in which Heyl critiques the writing in the note.

4. In groups, in writing, or in a general class discussion, have students respond to the worksheet on "It's a Crime Grammar Means Little to Robber."

"It's a Crime Grammar Means Little to Robber"

by Eric Heyl

Pittsburgh Tribune-Review (January 18, 2003)

Capable bank robbers seldom flub the holdup note. Like Olympic skaters who execute the challenging triple lutz, the successful bank robber does not botch that part of the presentation.

Jamie [name deleted] is not a successful bank robber.

The 18-year-old Peabody High School senior proved this Wednesday when she was charged with robbing the PNC Bank at Fifth Avenue Place, Downtown. She subsequently confessed to the crime.

The holdup note itself didn't lead to [the robber's] apprehension. Police found one of her fingerprints at the crime scene.

But had you seen the message before [she] presented it to the teller, you likely and accurately would have concluded she was destined for arrest. Concocting something as bad as the following isn't a good sign one has the ability to elude police:

> Put all the money in the bag that you could without making any noise or sudden movement that could cause you your life and your family's. Don't even think about putting any dye or anything that don't belong or I will see to it that you never make it home, so don't (expletive) with me.

Even in Pittsburgh, where the word "slippy" often is used to describe winter street conditions, most people probably would find [the] note atrociously constructed.

Ignore the run-on sentences if you can, but how do you ignore "*cause* you your life"? Similarly poor word choices found in high school English essays have been known to cost students passing grades.

The note orders the teller not to "put any dye," but it neglects to detail where not to put it. Likewise, while the teller was instructed not to "add anything that don't belong" (like what, a snow tire?), no specific mention is made of where not to add any inappropriate item.

There was one small plus for the poor teller who had to wade through this mess before forking over nearly $1,000 to [the robber]. The expletive was correctly spelled.

The length of [the robber's] holdup demand stands out from similar communiques. "They usually give very succinct instructions to the teller, like, 'Your money or else,'" said Jeff Killeen, a spokesman for the FBI's Pittsburgh office.

But grammar and usage errors such as the ones [the robber] committed can be found in even the briefest holdup note, according to Killeen.

"Not everyone who robs a bank has a bachelor's degree in English," he explained. "We don't see many bank robbers with post-high school educations. Maybe if they had them, they wouldn't be robbing banks."

George Fisher owns the Penn Aiken Dairy in Garfield, where [the robber] once worked. He gives the impression that [she] has the potential to craft significantly better holdup demands.

"She speaks very well. She's a little more clever than people give her credit for," Fisher said. Not quite clever enough to avoid her arrest last year for stealing more than $3,000 from the dairy, you understand, but still pretty clever.

It's nice Fisher speaks so highly of his larcenous ex-employee, but [the robber's] writing skills obviously need work. In addition to any criminal penalty she receives for robbing the bank, [she] should be sentenced to mandatory composition classes until she can consistently construct a grammatically correct holdup note.

She is guilty of assaulting the English language, and now she must pay the price. As [the robber] might put it, it's a classic example of cost and affect.

WORKSHEET ON "It's a Crime Grammar Means Little to Robber"

1. In his criticism of the bank robber's note, Heyl says, "Ignore the run-on sentences if you can. . . ." He obviously sees the note as having more than one run-on sentence. What is a run-on sentence? Look up "run-on sentence" in several grammar books and/or online at the Purdue Online Writing Lab (Google Purdue OWL), Grammar Girl's Quick and Dirty Tricks, or other grammar sites your instructor recommends. Does the robber's note contain run-ons?

2. Heyl says the robber's note is "atrociously constructed." What errors does she make? To what extent do you agree that the note is "atrociously constructed"?

3. Do you agree that she should have added more detail about where not to put the dye? Do you agree that she should have added more detailed instructions about where not to "add anything that don't belong"?

4. The robber's former boss seems to think that the robber was "a little more clever than people give her credit for." What does Heyl seem to think of the robber's intelligence? What makes you say that? How do you account for any discrepancy between the opinion the former boss has of the robber's intelligence and the columnist's opinion of her?

5. Does the columnist make any sentence errors?

6. What do you think of this topic as an amusing subject for this writer's column? What do you think of the columnist's tone? What makes you say that?

Answer Key for Worksheet

1. Most grammar books and online sites would disagree with Heyl that the bank robber's note contains run-on sentences. There should be a comma after *belong,* but the lack of one there does not make that sentence a run-on. The robber does use a co-coordinating conjunction, *or,* to separate the independent clauses. There are other errors in the note, but no run-ons.

2. She writes *could* instead of *can, don't* instead of *doesn't,* and *cause* instead of *cost.* But the two sentences are both constructed in consistent, imperative form. (Imperative sentences give commands.) She uses modifying phrases, apostrophes, and coordinating conjunctions correctly.

3. Answers will vary. However, the teller who received the demand managed to understand it enough to give the robber almost $1,000. In addition, the FBI spokesperson quoted later in the article seems to think the note was already too long.

4. The columnist seems to see a direct link between the errors in the bank robber's note and her intelligence. He also seems to go looking for errors in her writing, even, one might argue, making up errors that don't exist (run-ons). The robber's former boss, who knew her better, thinks she's much more intelligent than the columnist seems to think.

5. In the third paragraph from the end, there is a sentence fragment: "Not quite clever enough to avoid her arrest last year for stealing more than $3,000 from the dairy, you understand, but still pretty clever." This is most likely a deliberate fragment, constructed for stylistic purposes.

6. Answers will vary. Readers do seem to like to read about other people's spelling errors. Some students, however, might feel that given the seriousness of this news event (an adolescent girl being arrested for a felony and a bank teller probably terrified by the threat of violence), this humor column trivializes the experiences of both in order to get some cheap laughs. The tone seems to be snarky and self-righteous. (See, for example, the snow tire comment and the multiple insinuations that the bank robber is not very smart.)

Further Activities

1. In the same handbooks or websites in which you researched "run-on sentences," look up "sentence fragments." How are they defined? What is a "deliberate fragment"? What do these resources advise about using deliberate fragments?

2. In an *English Journal* article called "A Fresh Look at Sentence Fragments," long-time English teacher Edgar H. Schuster suggests that when texts are read quickly, many sentence fragments disappear because they actually work effectively for readers in some cases (2006, 79–80). He suggests that there are many forms of sentence fragment that are rhetorically valid and that they should be taught to high school and college students. Read Schuster's essay and discuss his new ideas for considering deliberate sentence fragments as valid forms of writing.

Lesson 2

Objectives

Students will:

- read for details
- read for inference
- think critically about choices news reporters make about the angle they take on what they report
- research newspaper articles on the Internet
- summarize and analyze the story and the angle it takes
- write a news story or letter to the editor, using appropriate genre conventions for each

Materials

- Handout: Scripps National Spelling Bee (p. 73)

Procedures

1. Five- to ten-minute warm-up: Ask students to choose from several of these questions and to write about them for two minutes and discuss them as a class:

   - What do you think is the purpose of a spelling bee?
   - If you were ever in a spelling bee in grade school, how did you study for it?
   - Once you were in the bee, how did it feel to spell a word correctly? to spell one incorrectly?
   - How important is it for a person to be able to spell correctly, without a spell-checker? Why?
   - How much time should be devoted in school to spelling?

2. Discuss.

3. Have students research and analyze news. (See handout.)

Handout: SCRIPPS NATIONAL SPELLING BEE

1. Check your local paper or use Google to find stories on the most recent Scripps National Spelling Bee (held in early June every year).

   a. If you're looking at a newspaper: Where in the paper did the story about the spelling bee appear? If it appeared on page 1, what other stories were also on page 1 that day? If you're looking online, what other stories seem to have equal weight? If you were the editor of that newspaper or website, would you place the spelling bee story in the same spot? Why or why not?

   b. What angle do reporters seem to take on these stories? Look at headlines, subheadings, lead sentences, and what most paragraphs focus on. Look for word connotations, too. Why do you think reporters chose that angle? What do you think of their decision to focus on that angle? What, if anything, does it reveal about our society that the reporters chose to focus on that angle?

2. Write a letter to the editor, praising or critiquing that paper's coverage of that year's Scripps National Spelling Bee. Or write a news story *about* the news stories you found.

Note: Instructors may enlist students to help generate criteria for evaluating these letters or news stories.

Further Activity

Examine the readers' comments that typically follow online articles about spelling or grammar or websites devoted to those topics. What assumptions do the commenters seem to hold? Do you agree with their apparent assumptions? Why or why not?

4

Grammar Rants on
Texting/Email Language

Background Information

These days, and for good reason, worries about teens texting and school
writing have shifted to concerns about the life-and-death issue of teens texting and driving. The initial concern—texting and the alleged attack on
English grammar—has mostly settled into two camps: those who see texting
as a bad influence on the writing of young people and those who see it as
simply another genre with its own conventions.

But in late April 2008, there was an explosion of newspaper articles and
columns that examined what was perceived as a crisis regarding that earlier
concern: widespread worry that teen writing for school was being unduly
influenced by text-messaging language. The spate of articles that appeared
at that time cited the Pew Internet & American Life Project, which had published its major study on April 24, 2008, "Writing, Technology and Teens"
(Lenhart et al. 2008). This seventy-one-page report was based on a national
telephone survey and focus group study of teens and their parents regarding
writing and electronic communication.

In this chapter, we examine some of those articles that made a story out
of that Pew report. We look at those stories and other rants about texting

and electronic language and how they fit with previous rants we've analyzed, which help us identify hidden societal assumptions about language, language change, young people, and morality.

Analyzing Grammar Rants About Texting

The day after the Pew report came out, Cynthia Hubert (2008) published a news story in *The Sacramento Bee*, "Teens Texting Symbols Invade Schoolwork : -(." The panicky tone of the headline, with its verb *invade*, continues in the lead: "OMG! The shortcuts and symbols that teenagers use in electronic conversations are creeping into their schoolwork!" (1). The verb *creeping* connotes something sneaky and evil, and *invade* in the headline connotes an enemy on the attack. The journalist feels free to use emoticons and texting language in her story, which is meant to be clever. And it fits the context of her real-world rhetorical situation. Although the style of the article appears more flexible, the article's content does not grant to students the kind of poetic license that Hubert gives herself.

Hubert uses another emoticon in her introduction to a quotation from a teacher she interviewed for the story: "Teachers are not necessarily :) about the trend" (2008, 1).

Interestingly, in the sentence immediately following this sentence, Hubert quotes a local teacher who provides no evidence of being unhappy about students using texting language. She says that students will sometimes use texting language in "little notes, but not in their formal work" (2008, 1).

Hubert is right that the Pew report says that a majority of students say they occasionally use some texting language in their schoolwork. She also says, near the end of her article, that most students report that texting language has no impact on their school writing (2008, 2). This is because, as Hubert herself mentions earlier on, students do not think of texting as "writing."

That is one of the main findings of the Pew report: that students do not think of texting as writing—a finding arguably worth far more exploration than it receives. Hubert, however, chose the texting-language-as-creeping-invader angle for her reporting on this study.

Someone skimming only Hubert's headline or her lead would completely miss whatever nuance she adds to the invading-texting-language angle: the teacher who doesn't think it's a problem and the vast majority of teens who don't see texting as impacting their writing. More importantly, someone reading only the headline or lead—or even Hubert's entire article—would miss what the writers of the Pew report thought was most important about their findings: that students do not think of texting as writing and that they do think writing is an important skill.

Hubert's piece accurately cites the Pew report, and nothing she says about the percentages of students who say texting language appears in their schoolwork is untrue. The story has a slant, though—an angle that seems to cherry-pick statistics from the report that support her headline and lead. She seems to want to raise alarms about texting language and schoolwork. And yes, the Pew report did address that issue. But texting language was not the main focus of the seventy-one pages. Here is the report's abstract that appears in large, bold print, immediately following the title, "Writing, Technology and Teens":

> Teens write a lot, but they do not think of their emails, instant and text messages as writing. This disconnect matters because teens believe good writing is an essential skill for success and that more writing instruction at school would help them. (Lenhart et al. 2008, i)

This emphasis in the original source continues. In the first paragraph of their introduction to the Pew report, the authors relate a number of interesting findings, only one of which addresses the texting-language-in-school-writing focus of Hubert's article. They report that "93% of teens say they write for their own pleasure," and that "Parents believe that their children write more as teens than they did at that age." In addition, students "also strongly believe that good writing is a critical skill to achieving success" (Lenhart et al. 2008, i–ii). These findings, each of which is newsworthy in its own right, are not foregrounded in the Hubert piece. Why? Perhaps it might take a bit more time to explain the implications of these statistics to readers, and they certainly don't fit neatly into the texting-as-enemy angle the reporter seems inclined to pursue.

Here is something else that was foregrounded in the Pew report, yet it was not something Hubert chose to highlight in her summary:

> Moreover, teens are filled with insights and critiques of the current state of writing instruction as well as ideas about how to make in-school writing instruction better and more useful. (Lenhart et al. 2008, ii)

In fact, two of the eight sections in the Pew report—twenty-two pages—go into some detail about those insights and critiques, including many suggestions

In the May 2009 *English Journal*, Kristen Hawley Turner published an article called "Flipping the Switch: Code-Switching from Text Speak to Standard English," in which she advocates effective ways of incorporating texting language into writing instruction.

students made about how the teaching of writing could be improved. Hubert might have featured that angle: students' views of how they thought writing instruction might be improved in the schools. But she chose instead to focus on Internet language "creeping" into school language and "invading" schoolwork.

Why not do a story on how the teaching of writing needs to change? Perhaps as they skimmed the Pew report, what caught Hubert and her editors' eye were statements and statistics that confirmed assumptions that already fit their views of texting, grammar, and students. Early in her report on the Pew study, Hubert highlights a quotation from a local high school senior she interviewed who has this to say about texting language: "I guess my generation is just super-lazy" (2008, 1).

Hubert was not the only reporter to stress the texting/schoolwork connection in the Pew Internet & American Life Project. In an article that appeared in *The New York Times*, Tamar Lewin had this headline: "Informal Style of Electronic Messages Is Showing Up in Schoolwork, Study Finds." And here is the lead: "As e-mail messages, text messages and social network postings become nearly ubiquitous in the lives of teenagers, the informality of electronic communication is *seeping* into their schoolwork, a new study says" (2008, 1; our emphasis). The next sentence summarizes the percentage of students who said their texting language "bled" into their schoolwork (1). Later in the article, Lewin mentions that students do not think of texting as real writing and also says a bit about how much students write, both in and out of school. But, like Hubert's story, this one clearly foregrounds the "seeping" or "bleeding" of texting language into schoolwork.

Two years after the Pew report was published, an article by Samantha Smithstein (2010) on the *Psychology Today* website (www.psychologytoday. com) continued to stress the "dangers" of texting in relation to "language and communication skills" (1), using the Pew report as a source. The article's title highlights these alleged dangers: "Too Easy to Say 'I h8 u' (and More Potential Pitfalls of Texting for Teens)." Later in her article, however, Smithstein cites more recent research from the British Academy that found that texting teens did better than their nontexting peers on spelling, reasoning, and "overall literacy." As with the Hubert article, however, anyone reading just the headline or just the lead of this piece would get a very skewed summary of the Pew report and would completely miss the summary of research that contradicted the reporter's headline and lead.

Journalists must always pick the angle they will take when covering a story. They can choose what they think will most interest their readers or will make the most dramatic headline. Because they are human, reporters naturally take from a published report the facts that pop out to them, given their individual interests and beliefs, even if they try to be as objective as possible. They may not even realize they are highlighting only a minor part of a report and neglecting what may be its most significant findings.

Students, however, as consumers of news stories, need to know how information becomes "news." By skimming the original Pew report (available online) and comparing the different published "takes" on what was significant about its findings, students can learn to think critically about who decides what is newsworthy, what facts are reported or not reported, what attitude the reporter seems to have toward the topic, and how headlines and lead sentences can be misleading.

Long before the 2008 Pew report was published, reporters and columnists were worried about text messaging and Internet language. As we saw in Hubert's article and in rants discussed in Chapter 1 on morality, laziness is a repeating theme when ranters complain about young people's language use.

For example, in April 2007, the *Western Courier* (published by Western Illinois University) ran a short opinion piece entitled "The Pitfalls of Text-Messaging." (See the marked-up grammar rant at end of this chapter.) Like many other grammar rants, this one begins with a claim that English is in danger. The new technology language "is putting the English language under attack. Something needs to be done about it." Here English is seen as an unchanging entity that shouldn't need or want new words, and furthermore, that someone should step up to fend off these attackers—as if there is an authority somewhere who is in charge of these things.

Before long, though, laziness surfaces: "Simply put, technology has made today's generation of students lazy by tempting them to take the easy way out when it comes to the English language." Technology is personified here, and it is the agent in the sentence. Technology is "tempting [students] to take the easy way out." Temptation, of course, is the primary occupation of Christianity's biggest villain, Satan. After praising France for trying to legislate what new words get to be admitted into the French language, the writer finishes the opinion piece by attacking "Internet lingo" and warning us that using it will have dire consequences: "today's youth will once again live up to the less-intelligent, lazy stereotype they have stamped on their foreheads."

A January 2010 BBC report written by Sean Coughlan discusses a British university study that shows children's ability to spell is not being negatively affected by frequent use of texting language. In fact, because texting language plays on conventional standards of spelling (for example, *l8tr* for *later*), the study suggests, use of texting might actually help students' development of standardized English spelling. (We thank Nancy Mack for sharing this information.)

We can infer a writer's attitude about language change even when the article is not an opinion piece but a news story. In a short piece about changes to a new dictionary, the headline to Simon Rabinovitch's (2007) article begins to reveal his view: "Thousands of Hyphens Perish as English Marches On." Here again, the inanimate beings—this time the hyphens—are the subject of the sentence, not the people who made the decisions regarding the new dictionary. The verb *perish* is usually reserved for human beings who die tragically through natural disasters or disease. Here is his lead: "About 16,000 words have succumbed to pressures of the Internet age and lost their hyphens in a new edition to the Shorter Oxford English Dictionary." In this sentence, too, words take center stage, not people. These words have "succumbed to pressures" and have "lost their hyphens." When people are finally the agents in a sentence, they are the dictionary team that "committed the grammatical amputations" (1). This little news story is just a filler, written in mock-heroic form for entertainment purposes. However, the writer seems to imply a distinct disapproval of changes to language. In addition to *perish* and *succumb,* other verbs throughout the article have negative connotations. Again, language changes that come from texting or Internet influences are seen as creeping intruders, infections that harm good, traditional English and make students lazy.

It's important for students to be able to distinguish between opinion pieces like columns and fact-based news stories such as front-page news, fillers, and features. Therefore, having students read short pieces representing a mix of these different genres helps them build not only background knowledge but also their awareness of different conventions. It's even more important for students to pay attention to *how* news and opinions are presented, to be aware of word connotation and of who or what the writer chooses to make the subject or agent of the sentence. It's good for students to become consciously aware of the reporter's angle and how closely that angle fits what others might see as the main point of, say, an original report being used as the main source for a news story. Students need to develop what Howard Schneider (2010), Dean of the School of Journalism at Stony Brook University, calls "news literacy." Columns and news stories reflect attitudes and assumptions in society, but they can also help shape those attitudes and assumptions, especially if readers are oblivious to the power of unexamined text to shape readers' views.

In the lessons section of this chapter, following the marked-up grammar rant, we suggest activities designed to develop students' close reading and inference skills, as well as a more sophisticated media literacy.

Marked-Up Grammar Rant

"The Pitfalls of Text-Messaging"

The Western Courier (April 2007; © Copyright 2009 Western Courier. Reprinted with permission)

On April 23, a 13-year-old girl won $25,000 by typing out "supercalifragilisticexpialidocious" in 15 seconds on a cellular phone. This was done as part of the national text-messaging championship.

Text-messaging, along with instant messaging, has slowly developed its own language and is putting the English language under attack. Something needs to be done about it

As the last generation before the instant messaging/text-messaging era, college students have seen firsthand what happens when technology takes over their lives.

Simply put, technology has made today's generation of students lazy by tempting them to take the easy way out when it comes to the English language.

> Notice how *text-messaging* is the subject of this sentence—the agent doing the action. It's not *people* who develop the new language; it's *text-messaging* itself, as if a mysterious, outside entity is "attacking" poor, vulnerable English.

> The definite article *the* used to modify English language is debatable. Is there really only one English language: *The* English language? Or are their many versions of English that function equally well in different contexts and for different purposes? Is texting language a version of English language, or is it an attack on *The* English language?

> Why would anyone call for language to be more complicated than it needs to be to serve its purpose? The point of most language is to communicate. If the communication works, what's wrong with it?

> Here is that very common theme in many grammar rants: *laziness*, the modern word for one of the seven deadly sins, sloth.

> The writer could have said: "We need to do something about it." What's the difference between "something needs to be done" and "we need to do something"?

> As we also saw in an earlier rant, *tempting* is a word often associated with the devil, or evil. And once again, it is *technology* that is doing this tempting, technology that is *acting upon* students.

> Again, technology is seen as the doer of the action, not college students who may choose to bring technology into their lives.

The author makes an important point here. There's nothing wrong with texting language in a place in which it works. Writers need to learn when to use it as well as how to use it.

This sentence seems to suggest that people who use texting language have no pride in their language.

This sentence seems to praise France, and its *Académie Française*, for barring any new or foreign words from entering the French language. The word *dedicated* is loaded with positive connotations, as is *pride*, in the previous sentence.

Text-messaging and instant messaging have become the primary form of conversation, taking away from using the telephone the old-fashioned way. Students, especially those who are in junior high, high school and occasionally college, are becoming so accustomed to "speaking" shorthand that it is moving from innocent conversation with friends to homework assignments and school papers.

It is understandable to use this shorthand for the sake of time and quick communication between friends, especially when some text-messaging charges are by the word. It's just a matter of being able to differentiate between leisurely conversations with friends and proper English rules.

Numerous countries throughout the world take pride in their languages, which have existed for thousands of years. Some countries, such as France, for example, are so dedicated to their language that they are hesitant to adopt new words into their vocabulary. In America, however, the word "jiggy" appears in several standard dictionaries.

It would seem the generation directly following ours has developed its own language, and there is no telling what will come of it in the future. If this trend continues, will words even be used, or will we revert back to cave paintings?

This sounds like the opposite of laziness.

This is a good example of extreme, "slippery slope" reasoning, which as Aristotle pointed out thousands of years ago, is not logically valid.

The word *however* seems to imply that the author does not approve of having this word appear in American dictionaries.

We should take pride in knowing correct grammar and how to read and write. By becoming so accustomed to using "Internet lingo," we will ◄ - - - - - - eventually transfer those words into the "real world," and today's youth will once again live up to the less-intelligent, lazy stereotype they have stamped on their foreheads.

> Another case of slippery-slope logic, which isn't a valid argument. Grammar ranters frequently predict dire outcomes from changes in language use.

> It's curious that one would be proud of the language they use, as if it's something to live up to. Language is a tool that serves a purpose. Of course, there is a logical consistency here in this article: if one should be ashamed of using bad grammar, then one should feel pride in using good grammar.

> Here's the laziness judgment again, as well as an added negative judgment regarding the intelligence of people who dare to use texting language outside the realm of text-messaging. (Why don't we hear the same complaints about sports "lingo" infecting the "real world"?)

Lesson 1

Objectives

Students will:

- hone close-reading skills, paying attention to word connotation
- understand how agency in a sentence—who or what is doing the action—contributes to meaning and emphasis
- think critically about the information they receive from news sources (by juxtaposing a reporter's summary of a research report with the researchers' own summary of their report)
- review the genre conventions of news stories and letters to editors

Materials

- Copy of Pew Report's abstract and summary
- Blackboard or overhead projection
- Handout 1: "Teens Texting Symbols Invade Schoolwork :-(." (p. 85)
- Handout 2: Questions on Pew Report (p. 87)

Procedures

1. Begin with this warm-up: Post on the board or screen a sentence written in typical texting language; for example, one of the following:

   Call me l8tr   (Call me later.)
   4GM   (Forgive me.)
   PAW CMB   (Parents are watching. Comment me back.)

   Then ask students: "Do you know what these texts mean? Do you think of texting language as 'writing'? Why or why not?" Discuss this for a few minutes. Then move on to Hubert's article.

2. Using a projection screen, overhead, or Handout 1, have students read the headline and lead of Cynthia Hubert's article (2008).

3. Give students Handout 1 and discuss.

4. Have students read the abstract of the study Hubert is reporting on (Lenhart et al. 2008). Then discuss Handout 2. If available, the first pages of the report might be projected for students to see what the original report looked like.

Handout 1

Headline: "Teens Texting Symbols Invade Schoolwork :-(."

Lead: OMG! The shortcuts and symbols that teenagers use in electronic conversations are creeping into their schoolwork! (by Cynthia Hubert, *The Sacramento Bee,* April 25, 2008)

1. From reading this headline and lead, what do you predict is the main focus of the research study Hubert is reporting on in this story?

2. Why can Hubert use texting abbreviations and emoticons in her news story?

3. What is the connotation of *invade*, used in the headline? How is *invade* usually used? What kinds of people or things usually *invade*?

4. What is the connotation of *creeping* in the lead sentence? How is *creeping* usually used? What kinds of people or things are usually depicted as *creeping*?

Answer Key for Handout 1

1. Hubert seems to focus on email language showing up in schoolwork.

2. Hubert can use texting language and emoticons with impunity because she has a certain amount of poetic license. Hubert and her editors obviously believe that her readers will "get" that she is including these texting symbols as a stylistic device. This published journalist is granted a poetic license that students writing for school typically are not granted. It may be that teachers or other authorities will not believe that a student's use of texting language is anything other than accidental or ignorant. Answers will vary as to whether or not this is fair.

3. *Invade* usually has a negative connotation: The enemy *invaded* the village. There was an *invasion* of cockroaches.

4. *Creeping* usually has a negative connotation: The lizards were *creeping* through the swamp. The burglar was *creeping* through the bushes. The zombies were *creeping* through the graveyard. That suspected criminal is a *creep*. The witch's raspy voice was *creepy*.

Handout 2: QUESTIONS ON PEW REPORT

Abstract of "Writing, Technology and Teens":

Teens write a lot, but they do not think of their emails, instant and text messages as writing. This disconnect matters because teens believe good writing is an essential skill for success and that more writing instruction at school would help them. (Lenhart et al. 2008)

1. From reading this abstract by the researchers, what do you predict was the main focus of this research?

2. Compare your predictions about what this report is about (based on this abstract) to your predictions about it based on Hubert's headline and lead.

Answer Key for Handout 2

1. The researchers themselves seem to focus much more than Hubert
and does on students not thinking of texting language as "writing." The
2. researchers also report that teens say they enjoy writing, especially
what they do outside of school, and that they have many ideas on
how writing instruction could be improved. Answers will vary as to
what students' predictions were, but Hubert's headline and lead
seem to focus on texting language appearing in school writing. Why
Hubert, like other journalists who reported on this research, chose to
focus on the "invasive" quality of texting language is an open question. Perhaps she holds a common assumption that "correctness" is
universal, even across different contexts and genres. Perhaps she's
against language change.

Optional Activities

If time permits, also have students read the first and last paragraphs of the
Pew researchers' "Summary of Findings" (Lenhart et al. 2008):

First paragraph of researchers' "Summary of Findings":

> Teenagers' lives are filled with writing. All teens write for school, and 93%
> of teens say they write for their own pleasure. Most notably, the vast
> majority of teens have eagerly embraced written communication with
> their peers as they share messages on their social network pages, in
> emails and instant messages online, and through fast-paced thumb choreography on their cell phones. Parents believe that their children write
> more as teens than they did at that age.

Last paragraph of researchers' "Summary of Findings":

> At the same time that teens disassociate e-communication with "writing,"
> they also strongly believe that good writing is a critical skill to achieving
> success—and their parents agree. Moreover, teens are filled with insights
> and critiques of the current state of writing instruction as well as ideas
> about how to make in-school writing instruction better and more useful.

Questions for Discussion

1. From reading the first and last paragraphs of the researchers' own summary of their seventy-one-page report, what else do you learn about what they discovered?

2. What do *you* think is most important about what they found? Why?

3. Compare Hubert's summary of the report (as indicated in her headline and lead) to the researchers' own summary of it.

4. Compare what Hubert seems to emphasize to what you would emphasize.

5. How do you account for any differences you find between what Hubert emphasizes and what the researchers themselves emphasize, or what you would emphasize?

Further Activities or Research Projects

- Have a debate regarding the pros and cons of text messaging and writing. To what extent does texting hurt communication and school-work? To what extent does it help communication or help writers shift between different conventions required for different genres?
- Write a letter to English teachers in which you describe what beliefs about texting language should be taught and learned in school.
- Write a brief news story, summarizing the results of a recent, well-known, published report and interviewing several local experts on the issue. Instructors might wish to first briefly review the news story genre, examining several short examples and discussing their elements and conventions. News stories have leads, which quickly summarize the who, what, when, where of a story, and they are supposed to be timely. (The publication of the Pew report on April 24, 2008, made Hubert's April 25 article on teen texting and writing very timely.) News stories also typically report on brief interviews with real people, such as the students and teachers mentioned in the Hubert

article. They usually include a combination of indirect and direct quotations, as Hubert's does. A review of interviewing techniques and paraphrasing and correctly punctuating quotes (for the news story) might also be helpful.

- Read several news stories covering a recently published research report, and then read the original report yourself. What do the reporters stress in their stories? What would you stress? Write a letter to the editor either commending the coverage the research report received or raising questions about how the research was covered in the news story. Instructors might review genre conventions for letters to the editor, examining several short examples and discussing their elements and conventions.

- Research the study Smithstein (2010) cites from the British Academy (2010) that found that texting teens did better than their nontexting peers on spelling, reasoning, and literacy. One academic piece on this topic is Beverly Plester and Clare Wood's (2009) article, "Exploring Relationships Between Traditional and New Media Literacies: British Preteen Texters at School." Or, find more research on this topic and reach your own conclusions based on a variety of research results.

Lesson 2

Objectives

Students will:

- read for details and comprehension
- identify active verbs and analyze the connotations of such verbs
- think critically about a writer's choice to use verbs with particular connotations and what those connotations suggest about the writer's slant on this issue
- learn how language change happens over time and how "rules" about language change

Materials

- Internet access
- Handout: Short Articles Covering Hyphen Loss in New Oxford English Dictionary (p. 92)
- *Optional:* Access to Bryan A. Garner's (2009) reference book, *Garner's Modern American Usage*

Procedures

1. Begin with brief motivation or warm-up activity. Ask students orally: "How do you spell *bumble bee*?" Write on board: "Is it *bumble bee, bumble-bee,* or *bumblebee*? Who decides? How?" Discuss.

2. Explain that in the fall of 2007, the editors of the Shorter Oxford English Dictionary made a number of changes to the new edition. They eliminated the hyphen from thousands of words (including from *bumble-bee*). Some previously hyphenated words became two words; others became one word. This news sparked many short feature news stories about the loss of hyphens.

3. Have students google the following phrase: "hyphens Oxford English Dictionary, September 2007."

4. Have students select and read a number of short articles or news features that come up in the search.

5. Have students read the handout questions and discuss them.

6. If time permits, complete the further activities.

Handout: SHORT ARTICLES COVERING HYPHEN LOSS IN NEW OXFORD ENGLISH DICTIONARY

1. Underline the verbs used in the headlines, leads, and several paragraphs of the articles you found covering the elimination of many hyphens. What are some of these verbs? What connotations do they have? For example, some verbs from Simon Rabinovitch's (2007) article, "Thousands of Hyphens Perish as English Marches On," include: *perish, succumb, lost.* How is *succumbed* usually used? Who or what usually *succumbs*? What about *perish*? Who or what usually *perishes*? How? To find out, check a comprehensive dictionary, or see the sample sentences for *perish* that illustrate context. What does a writer's use of verbs in these articles imply about his or her view of language change?

2. What did you learn in the articles you found about how hyphens are removed from words? What research is done, and by whom, before hyphens are removed from words in a dictionary? What does this tell you about how "correct" and "incorrect" forms of English language are determined?

Answer Key for Handout

1. Verbs used in these articles include: *perish, succumbed, lost,* and so on. In common usage, it is usually a person who *succumbs* to something like an illness or a disease or *perishes* from a fire, a flood, or a disease. If people usually succumb to illness or perish in floods or disease epidemics, and now we have hyphens perishing, succumbing, or getting lost, the changes in the dictionary are being subtly linked with disease and death. Although the mock-heroic nature of some of these articles may just be the writers having fun, it may also be that they disapprove of language change. Certainly some of these articles could be used to perpetuate a conservative view of language shift.

2. The team does not simply make arbitrary rulings on language. Theirs is a descriptive method, not a prescriptive one. They look at words and sentences that appear in recent books or newspapers, or online. In other words, they are guided by what is already happening in contemporary usage. They don't impose arbitrary standards; they identify how language is actually being used in the real world and then they use those real-world uses to set a more formalized standard.

Further Activities, Homework Suggestions, and Research/Writing

- Compare old and new dictionaries regarding these and other words to see what's changed. Compare old and new grammar handbooks regarding the spelling of hyphenated words. Have all new dictionaries followed the lead of the Shorter Oxford English Dictionary?
- Read the entry on hyphens in *Garner's Modern American Usage* (Garner 2009) (under Punctuation, and then J. Hyphen, p. 679). What are "phrasal adjectives"?
- Research how words come to be added or eliminated from dictionaries.
- Read the preface to the first, second, and third edition of Bryan Garner's book, *Garner's Modern American Usage* (Garner 2009). (All three are published in the third edition [xi–xxii].) Another excellent essay in that same edition is "Making Peace in the Language Wars" (xxxvii–xlix).

5

The Grammar Trap

What's a Writer to Do?

Background Information

Fill in the correct possessive pronoun in the blank below:

Each student should bring _____ book to class.

What is the missing word? When we've asked this question in our classes, we've received the following answers: *his, her, his or her, her or his, his/her, their*. The correct answer is that they are all wrong. It's a trap. If your reader has more power than you and that reader expects one of the above answers, you will be wrong if you don't select it. The answer *his* is a leftover from the time when *he* was considered the "universal gender." There are still plenty of old-fashioned readers out there—many of whom have power—who continue to enforce this largely outdated rule. The use of *her* in the blank is occasionally expected by those who seek to give equal time back to the female gender, while still others expect the pronoun to shift gender within an essay, every other paragraph, again to give equal time. The answer *his or her* is probably the most common answer we get, but there are some who consider it awkward or unnecessarily wordy. *His/her* with a slash is generally disliked, but those who find *his or her* too wordy sometimes prefer it. *S/he* is another slash that we occasionally see in print, but that is almost always disliked. Finally, using the word *their* in the sentence above eliminates the gender issue, but it requires treating the plural pronoun *they* as if it were singular. Some readers detest this and consider it the height of ignorance and proof of the downfall of civilization. Others read right over it with no problem, as it doesn't interfere with meaning. And, since the word *you* can be singular or plural and it doesn't denote gender, there is precedent. Still others find that the best thing to do is to revise the sentence so that a plural pronoun is appropriate: "All students should bring their books to class." The problem here is that sometimes a writer wants to use the singular construction for emphasis.

With all these options available, making any choice to fill in a sentence like this is essentially a trap. So what are writers to do? Writers must get to know the readers they are writing for and what their preferences are—especially if that audience has some form of power over them. In many cases, the writer can't find out the audience's preferences for this level of minutia, so the writer simply has to take a best guess. It's a gamble. And as with all gambling, sometimes the writer will lose. So we recommend that a writer try not to be a perfectionist with his or her own writing and to forgive others when their best guess about a grammar trap situation is different from the one he or she would have chosen.*

Even the most informed, careful proofreader may be the target of more powerful, less informed ranters who are quite comfortable making nasty insinuations about the intelligence or morality of a writer based on an extra apostrophe or comma. To protect themselves against the most venomous attacks, students must be able to proofread their papers carefully, and they need a working familiarity with the kinds of minor errors that most upset ranters. However, as we have seen, some of the rules ranters recite may not be rules at all, but stylistic preferences, or the rule may have numerous exceptions not listed by lecturing ranters. Such ranters may trumpet outdated conventions or house style preferences that don't fit the writer's context.

At this point, instructors might be thinking, "Where does all this leave us? What *should* we be teaching our students?" Naturally, we want our students to be able to avoid the wrath of grammar ranters, who may be their professors, potential employers, supervisors, or others with authority. At the same time, we want students to write with at least some of the informed sophistication that professional writers enjoy. We want students to adjust

---

* We would like to thank Lisa Luedeke, who came up with the concept of the Grammar Trap.

their style to fit the context and conventions of the genre they're writing in. But we also want them to be engaged enough in their writing to stretch that genre in imaginative ways if they want to, the way real writers do as they develop a style. Obviously, students should know whatever rules will help them. But they should also know the backstory on those rules: what those rules are really based on (logic, cultural habit, personal preference, etc.); how those rules have changed over the years; how they come to change; how context and writer's authority influence adherence to those rules; and how grammar handbooks may disagree with each other about those rules.

Therefore, students should analyze grammar rants. Doing so will first of all draw students' attention to whatever editing detail the ranter is fretting about, so that they can avoid that problem. And, by analyzing grammar rants—examining their metaphors, unpacking their connotations, and questioning their implications—students will get both a close-up view and a bird's-eye view of language controversies, without being directly involved. This way, students will learn about the grammatical rules that matter for them without personally experiencing the confidence-busting insults they could suffer if these rants were about their own writing.

Won't all this just confuse students? On the contrary. The human drama involved will draw them into the controversy, helping them pay attention to language and what is said about it. By having a chance to research and investigate the ranters' claims, students will build the knowledge and authority they need to take control of their language choices.

Yes, writers need to know "grammar rules," to the extent that those rules can help them compose and proofread successful writing. But they also need a desire to write and some modicum of hope they'll be successful at it. They need a way to generate ideas, and they need a reader interested in those ideas, not just one ready to pounce on real or imagined mistakes. When students acquire the background in language to judge the judges, they will learn much about that language. They will also learn to analyze text, to evaluate claims, and to think critically.

In the remainder of this chapter, we survey the territory of several other grammar traps: language contexts in which there is no single correct answer that everyone agrees upon. We examine more about pronouns, apostrophes, run-on sentences, and sentence fragments. Learning more about these traps may help writers become more sensitive to the need to make careful grammatical choices and may help readers become a little less persnickety about their own grammatical preferences.

Pronouns, Human Life, and Public Policy

In April 2010, First Lady Michelle Obama visited Haiti to witness the devastation caused by the 7.0 earthquake that hit that country in January and to monitor progress in helping at least two million now-homeless citizens put their lives back together. More than 200,000 people were killed by that quake. Back in the United States, blogs were written that focused on Mrs. Obama's use of pronouns during her visit. (She said "for Jill and I" instead of "for Jill and me.") This stunning attention to grammar trivia at a time of such widespread human misery says much about our society and some people's intense interest in other people's language use.

Blogger Joan Gage had this to say about Mrs. Obama's statement in Haiti:

> You don't expect perfect grammar from a baseball player . . . but maybe you do from a First Lady who's a lawyer, educated at Princeton and Harvard.
>   Kids acquire an ear for correct grammar by hearing it spoken by the adults around them.

The insult to baseball players notwithstanding, Gage's concern here about children's role models is ironic. The unspoken message in her blog entry is that even in the face of untold human suffering caused by a devastating earthquake, pronoun use is an appropriate topic on which to focus.

This complaint about errors involving the nominative or objective case of pronouns is but one in a series of published complaints on this issue. In mid-December 2008, then President-elect Barack Obama nominated Arne Duncan to be the next Secretary of Education. In a statement following this nomination, Mr. Duncan said many things. However, the thirty-three-second video clip of his speech that dominated blog sites for days contained the following phrase, which grammar ranters gleefully foregrounded:

> He gave my sister and I the opportunity to start a great school. . . .

On December 16, 2008, many bloggers pointed out—usually in their very first sentence about Duncan's long speech—that Duncan should have said, "He gave my sister and *me*. . . ." A column on the Politico.com blog (December 16, 2008) had this headline: "Did the New EdSec Just Make a Grammar Error?" (Cullen 2008). And Gawker, at Gawker.com, had this one: "Our Stupid New Education Secretary Said Something Stupid!" (Pareen 2008). Columnist June

Blogger Joan Gage says, "You don't expect perfect grammar from a baseball player," but her fellow grammar ranter, Jim Nelson, writing in the *Bluefield Daily Telegraph*, criticizes the Texas Rangers' Michael Young for ending a sentence "with two consecutive prepositions." (See Chapter 2.) Is no one safe from the wrath of grammar ranters?!

Casagrande (2009) devotes her entire essay ("A Word Please") in the *Kilgore News Herald* to Duncan's error, providing readers with a detailed lesson on how to use pronouns and ending her column with this concluding sentence: "And that's why, in an acceptance speech for the job of education secretary of the United States, Duncan should have demonstrated a grasp of subject and object pronouns."

Ranters seem to relish errors of this kind made by President Obama, Secretary of Education Arne Duncan, the First Lady, or just about anyone whose quoted or recorded words can then become the subject of someone else's unsolicited lesson. These ranters seem thrilled at the chance to point out an error made by someone in power, much like children shrieking with delight when a parent knocks over a glass of milk (or when a teacher misspells something on the blackboard).

These blogs and columns on the nominative and objective case of pronouns can be helpful to writers for several reasons. First, students can witness the effect such minor errors have on readers, readers who don't even claim these errors are confusing. Second, writers who wish to avoid such condemnations of their own writing can briefly review the rules on nominative and objective case pronouns, which are fairly clear.

Some students might observe, however, that parents' and teachers' repeated reminders to children to say "My sister and *I* went to the store," instead of "My sister and *me*," might be partially responsible for the seemingly knee-jerk avoidance of objective case pronouns, even when they are warranted. In other words, previous corrections may have worked too well. The phrase, "my sister and I" may begin to sound more correct, even "more formal" in *all* situations than does "my sister and me," which we may have been too successfully scolded out of using ever.

Students might also wish to note that Bryan Garner, in his highly respected style guide, *Modern American Usage* (2009), adds a caveat to the rules about pronouns and case. He notes that in some constructions involving pronouns, writers deliberately use an incorrect form: "Occasionally, writers avoid the strictly correct form merely to avoid seeming pedantic" (664). He discusses what is technically correct and what is commonly done for stylistic reasons in magazines such as *Newsweek* and *Harper's* magazine. These facts can help students think about how writers in the real world make the decisions they do based on their audience, purpose, genre, and context. Finally, exploring all aspects of these grammar rants on the speeches of famous people can send students back to the speaker's original transcript,

When a mistake in language results from applying a correction of another error to a different case, linguists call this "hypercorrection." So, for example, when a speaker trying to use standardized English mistakenly uses "John and I" in a situation that requires the objective case ("for John and me," "invited John and me," "to John and me," etc.), it may result from hypercorrecting "John and me" when that phrase is mistakenly used in the nominative case: "John and me went to the store" *should* be "John and I went to the store."

exposing them to thought-provoking social and educational issues. Doing so may also get them thinking critically about the choices bloggers make when they rant about pronouns instead of about important problems discussed in statements by powerful policy makers.

The Serial Comma Trap

A controversy over the serial comma (also called the *Oxford comma* and the *Harvard comma*) is particularly illustrative. People rant about it on the Internet, inquire about it to advice columnists, and wave in others' faces whichever grammar handbook happens to support their view of what's correct. The crux of this crisis? The number of commas that belong in the following sentence.

I bought apples bananas and pears.

Those who say one comma are on one side of this standoff; those who say two belong to the serial/Oxford/Harvard comma crowd. Which is the "right" answer? The handbooks, especially the most respected, most frequently consulted ones, don't agree.

In one corner, we have the venerable Strunk and White text, *The Elements of Style* (2005), familiar to most English teachers, which says, in its typically no-nonsense way, that the serial comma should be used: "In a series of three or more terms with a single conjunction, use a comma after each term except the last" (3). In the other corner, we have the mighty *AP Style Book* (Christian, Jacobsen, and Minthorn 2009), used by journalists writing for the Associated Press. That book supports the "apples, bananas and pears" approach to words in a series: no comma before the conjunction *and* (355). People fight about this because they're citing different handbooks (or quoting former teachers who used different handbooks as their authorities).

Of course, there are some issues here related to clarity and to the avoidance of ambiguity. Everyone agrees that writers should add whatever commas they need to make their sentence clear. But if that last comma in the series is not absolutely needed for clarity, people will fight tooth and nail about "the rule."

Bud and Tiffany Hunt show how the serial comma controversy plays out on the Internet. They note that when they googled "serial comma," they found 27,000 listings for that topic (2006, 89). (At this writing, it's up to 95,100!) As the Hunts point out, Wikipedia's entry on the serial comma is a gem. When we visited that site, it had all kinds of helpful links, including links to style guides in favor of, and against, the serial comma. There's a link to a poem about the serial comma and one to a 2008 alternative rock song called "Oxford Comma," the first line of which is "Who gives a f**k about an Oxford Comma?" There's also a student group on Facebook called "Students for the Preservation of the Oxford Comma," which has almost four thousand members.

It's fun to see how different handbooks weigh in. The *Little, Brown Compact Handbook* (Aaron 2007) states, "the final comma is never wrong" (270). Strunk and White's sage volume, *The Elements of Style*, adds a caveat to its endorsement of the serial comma: "In the names of business firms the last comma is usually omitted. Follow the usage of the individual firm" (2005, 3). We think that's a good suggestion: to punctuate a company the way it punctuates itself.

One of the sanest takes on this particular comma drama comes from John B. Bremner's *Words on Words*:

> Newspapers and other popular publications usually don't use a comma before *and* in a series. Scholarly publications usually do. Kate L. Turabian, author of *A Manual for Writers of Term Papers, Theses, and Dissertations*, an authoritative stylebook for academic research, insists on the comma before *and* in a series and she must have been pained when the front cover of the fifteenth impression of her work dropped the comma after *Theses* in the title. (1980, 104)

We see, therefore, what this controversy mostly boils down to is this: Because a sentence with the final comma takes up a bit more ink than does a sentence without that comma before the conjunction, newspapers have traditionally *not* used the serial comma, unless they really do need it for clarity. This convention (no serial comma) is reflected in the style book widely used by journalists, the *AP Style Guide*. Most other writers in the United States *do* use the serial comma because they are using style guides that support its use: Strunk and White's *The Elements of Style* (2005), the *MLA Handbook* (Gibaldi 1999), and many college handbooks, though most of them mention something about the slipperiness of the rule. Therefore, teachers preaching about (or students searching for) one, final, irrefutable rule about using a comma in a series are on a fool's errand. A more productive pursuit would focus on the genre, context, and audience for the piece.

This sniping about the serial comma is a bit like the Northern and Southern hemispheres arguing about which months of the year are summer or whether the water goes down the drain clockwise or counterclockwise. The "right" answer depends on whether you happen to be standing north or south of the equator, just as the "rightness" of the serial comma depends on which handbook or style sheet the particular class, school, office, publisher, college, or company is using. The lesson for students is not to learn "the rule" about commas in a series—because there are two rules, not including their exceptions. The way to avoid this trap is to scope out the rhetorical situation in which the question arises and answer it in the manner most likely to be effective in that situation (or the least likely to be ineffective, if it's an especially tricky one).

Apostrophe Traps

There are other, equally minute issues that greatly upset people. Bonnie Rosenstock (2005) has written an interesting article in *The Villager* with this headline: "The Great St. Marks/Mark's Punctuation Debate Solved." Here's the problem: in the East Village in New York City is an area known as St. Mark's Place (or St. Marks Place), wherein the businesses all use different ways of punctuating themselves.

According to Rosenstock's research, there is a St. Marks Hotel (no apostrophe), a St. Mark's Comics and St. Mark's Bookshop (both *with* the apostrophe), and a St. Marks Ale House (without apostrophe). Punctuation differences about names of other establishments continue in that vein throughout this stretch of the Village, including how residents punctuate their home address (St. Mark's Place or St. Marks Place).

Rosenstock tells us about the woes of the Pearl Theater Company, whose address is announced on a big sign reading "80 St. Marks." For ten years, the repertory company's letterhead has had an apostrophe in its address. But the new marketing director, Matt Schicker, thought this situation was untenable and began a campaign to have the apostrophe eradicated, so that the letterhead now matches the big overhead sign on the building. Rosenstock quotes the old marketing director, Matthew Coleman: "It destroyed my world, knowing that I've been wrong for the five years I've been here. We're in the process of great reform. I still have to stop, proofread and change everything to without an apostrophe. It was a passionate debate for a while" (Rosenstock

2005, 2). The article continues for two more pages chronicling similar crises in this area. There were inquiries made to *The New York Times*, the New York Historical Society, and the Department of Transportation, all in a (failed) effort to resolve the issue.

In a raging debate similar to the one that took place in New York's East Village, citizens of Birmingham, England, fought for years about whether one of their suburbs, Kings Heath, should have an apostrophe (Associated Press 2009). The Birmingham City Council finally decided to ban the apostrophe on all their road signs. A spokesperson from the Plain English Campaign called the decision "complete lunacy," and the founder of the Apostrophe Protection Society, John Richards, said, "Now children will go around Birmingham and see utter chaos" (Adams 2009). A recent Google search on "apostrophes and Birmingham" yielded almost 100,000 hits.

The Run-On and Fragment Trap

Other hot-button issues for readers concern run-ons and fragments. Writers should be aware that for some readers, finding one run-on or one fragment in a piece of writing makes the readers lose all respect for the writer, especially if that writer is a student. Like conventions surrounding pronouns and apostrophes, however, rules governing these departures from correctness also bring with them exceptions not often highlighted when ranters are on a roll.

Here's what David Lynn says in *Education Digest* about the run-on: "A run-on sentence (also known as a comma splice) blurs connections and breeds confusion" (1993, 69).

In most grammar handbooks, the *run-on* sentence is equated with the *fused* sentence (independent clauses joined with no punctuation between them, as in, "The car was totaled we had to get a rental"). In some handbooks, no doubt the one David Lynn is used to, the run-on includes *both* fused sentences and comma splices (two independent clauses joined with a mere comma, which is not enough).

Fused sentence (run-on):

The car was totaled we had to get a rental.

Comma splice (also called run-ons, in some grammar books):

The car was totaled, we had to get a rental.

Granted, the sentence "The car was totaled, we had to get a rental." would be deemed incorrect by most handbooks and English teachers. But it is hardly confusing. The connections are quite clear. The independent clauses in it should probably be divided by a semicolon, or by a comma and a conjunction such as *and*, or the comma splice should simply be divided into two separate sentences. Because the connection between the two clauses is obvious, however, and the presence of a mere comma instead of a semicolon does not leave readers totally befuddled, then David Lynn's use of such exaggerated language ("blurs connections and breeds confusion") suggests that there must be something else going on.

As Joseph Williams (1981) has demonstrated, reaction to error (or perceived error) depends on who is reading whose writing. A reader with more power or prestige than the writer (say, a teacher reading a student's essay) is much more likely to both notice the comma splice and to be annoyed by it. A reader with less power or prestige than the writer (say, a fan reading a Pulitzer Prize–winning writer's fiction) is less likely to even notice the comma splice, let alone be annoyed by it. However, instructors reading students' essays usually demand a much more rigid adherence to rules and perceived rules about the comma splice than do readers of famous writers' fiction. What about the rules? Even the thickest, oldest, most widely respected handbooks outline some exceptions to the "rules" about run-ons. Fragments, too, have some complex guidelines.

Here is what David Lynn says about sentence fragments: "Unless used for deliberate effect, incomplete sentences, lacking a subject or predicate, can baffle sense altogether." Lynn provides no examples of deliberate fragments or who gets to use them. And although some fragments are certainly confusing, it's doubtful that most of them "baffle sense altogether" (1993, 68–69).

We're not saying that Lynn is wrong to try to get students to fix comma splices or fused sentences. A semicolon between the two independent clauses in a run-on would certainly be less distracting to some readers—though writers should be aware that some readers mistakenly think any long sentence is a run-on. And students, especially, should be careful with sentence fragments because they cannot rely on their readers to know when such fragments are deliberate. But the histrionic language surrounding simple fragments and run-ons ("the very picture of intellectual hiatus," says Peter Kalkavage [1998, 59]) is itself worth analyzing.

As does Lynn, most complainers about run-ons and comma splices cite lack of clarity or even confusion as the reason they are so upset by the sentence error. But even in most examples of run-ons and commas splices used in handbooks, the confusion allegations don't hold up. Few readers would actually be confused by the lack of a semicolon or other legitimate divider of the independent clauses making up the sample bad sentences in the handbooks. Many ranters, however, have an intense emotional reaction to this sentence error.

If students are paying attention to sentences published in the real world, exaggerated critiques of run-ons and fragments might themselves be confusing. For example, if students were to write a sentence such as the one below, penned by Pulitzer Prize–winner Annie Proulx, oh boy, would the red ink flow!

> Eugenie felt the blood rise in her face, her heart thrummed with hatred for the pink-chopped doctor, whose eyes were bright with malice and who obviously relished the news he was breaking. (Proulx 2004, 105)

It's not the "pink-chopped doctor" or "thrummed" that would raise eyebrows—well, maybe a few. What sticks out, punctuation-wise, is the combining of two independent clauses with a mere comma. This sentence by Annie Proulx might indeed be called a comma splice, one of the most hated errors among people who notice such things. Proulx's frequent use of the stylistic comma splice has to do with the genre she's writing in—fiction—which generally allows more flexibility in style than do genres such as essay exams, news stories, or research papers of the kind written in school. Instead of a simplistic "c/s" mark on their paper when they use a comma splice, students should be brought in on the brouhaha comma splices can set off. They should also be brought in on the differences in genre, social status, and power difference between reader and writer that makes it okay for some writers to use comma splices but makes them punishment-deserving errors for others.

Walter H. Johnson, for example, explains in his extended grammar rant in the *English Journal* how the presence of one comma splice in a student's paper can bring it from an A to a C. He shows no mercy, showcasing his college's department-wide policy on error:

> Any student paragraph or essay that contains *one* sentence error (comma splice, fused sentence, or fragment) cannot receive a grade higher than a C; two such errors result in a D, and three or more result in an automatic F. (2006, 14; our emphasis)

If Annie Proulx were to produce for Johnson's class her sentence we looked at above, she'd get a C on her essay, and that's if she produced only *one* comma splice. The gist of Johnson's argument is that because his English department's punishment for committing a run-on is so high for students, there should be "universal agreement" (15) on what constitutes the rule for run-ons. He never suggests that perhaps the punishment for perceived errors should be modified. He goes on to rant about the handbooks and professional writers that depart from rules he'd like to see as fixed, once and for all.

Johnson complains about writing in the real world that takes "liberties" with grammar (2006, 14). Here he means the kinds of sentences Annie Proulx and many other published writers create that some might call run-ons or comma splices. He also hunts down fragments. He goes on to scold "modern college-level grammar handbooks" for "not helping the cause for sentence-structure correctness." He singles out several handbooks for taking these "liberties" with the rules and allowing such things as "intentional fragments" and "acceptable comma splices" (14).

To be fair to Johnson, in his rant he does say that he would accept a deliberate fragment, if a student were to point it out, but then he immediately adds this caveat: "but encouraging this liberty detracts from the emphasis we place on the control we demand over sentence structure correctness" (2006, 14). But an effective deliberate fragment in an appropriate genre is not a "liberty." It can be an informed, stylistic choice that demonstrates control. Young writers cannot learn this control, however, if they are taught only part of a rule and not its exceptions, or if they are punished so severely for one or two errors (that aren't even errors to everyone) that they lose any interest or excitement they might once have had about writing.

We will return to Johnson's rant about sentence punctuation, but let's take a look at some of the many handbooks (not the ones he mentions), old and new, that take this "liberty."

The Harper Handbook of College Composition (Third Edition), published in 1952, begins its section on the comma splice, which it also refers to as the "comma fault" and the "illiterate comma," with some tough talk in its definition:

> With either label, the *unjustifiable comma splice* is a serious error which causes confusion to the reader, since the writer does not show him where one sentence ends and the other begins. (Wykoff and Shaw 1952, 275; our emphasis)

This handbook calls the comma splice something that causes confusion, yet the examples it uses to illustrate this "serious error" are not confusing at all:

A meeting of the Botany Club will be held on Friday evening, several important matters are to be discussed.

Father's office is on the 35th floor, it overlooks the Hudson River. (Wykoff and Shaw 1952, 275)

Those two examples are, indeed, comma splices. And Walter Johnson would certainly see them as serious errors that cause confusion. The handbook excerpt above refers briefly to an "*unjustifiable*" comma splice (emphasis added), which implies there are justifiable ones. Several pages later, the *Harper Handbook* discusses such things.

Finally, to illustrate the distinctly *not* modern feature of this handbook, note the reference to the reader as "him." The vast majority of grammar handbooks written since about 1980 would have used the more inclusive "him or her" to refer to the reader. But when this handbook was published, in 1952, the masculine pronoun was still an acceptable convention, as was the blithe use of "Father's office" in the examples, with no examples suggesting that Mother might have had an office that overlooks the Hudson. Current controversies regarding gendered pronouns are also worth exploring, but what is noteworthy here is how the mid-twentieth-century historical context influenced the word choice.

Walter H. Johnson, complaining above about "modern" handbooks daring to take "liberties" with what he calls "sentence-structure correctness" (2006), might be surprised at what this musty 1952 *Harper Handbook* has to say: "Use a justifiable comma splice when it is appropriate and effective." This senior citizen of handbooks even has "rules" about when the comma splice is, indeed, "justifiable":

1. *When the independent clauses are very short, with the subjects usually the same.*

    I came, I saw, I conquered. (Julius Caesar's famous sentence)

    You do work hard, you should work even harder.

    Mother obeys signs, she is a careful driver.

2. *When the independent clauses, neither one very long, express contrast.* (Wykoff and Shaw 1952, 278; italics in original)

The explanation continues. Here is one of their examples:

> This is Henry, that is George. (Wykoff and Shaw 1952, 278)

One of the most famous handbooks, Strunk and White's *Elements of Style*, says, in no uncertain terms: "Do not join independent clauses with a comma" (2005, 11). They recommend joining them with a semicolon or splitting the independent clauses into two sentences. However, they also write:

> An exception to the semicolon rule is worth noting here. A comma is preferable when the clauses are very short and alike in form, or when the tone of the sentence is easy and conversational.
>
> > Man proposes, God disposes.
> > The gates swing apart, the bridge fell, the portcullis was drawn up.
> > I hardly knew him, he was so changed.
> > Here today, gone tomorrow. (Strunk and White 2005, 12)

Note how Strunk and White even say "a comma is *preferable*" (emphasis added) in certain situations. There is judgment and interpretation involved. The clauses must be "very short and alike in form," or "the tone of the sentence is easy and conversational." One wonders who gets to make those judgments: the writers or the readers?

There are undoubtedly fairly consistent published rules for avoiding comma splices. There are also, published in some of those same handbooks, exceptions to those rules. However, the exceptions often require judgment or interpretation. Most grammar ranters have a "one right answer" approach to knowledge and are uncomfortable with interpretation.

By now, instructors and students alike have probably heard more than they've ever wanted to hear about comma splices and run-ons. But because the "comma splice" is high on readers' lists of pet peeves, writers might wish to investigate further what it is and what it isn't, and who can write a "justifiable comma splice" and who cannot. The most succinct advice regarding the comma splice comes from Lynne Truss in *Eats, Shoots & Leaves*. She says, "Only do it if you're famous" (2003, 88).

In the section following the marked-up grammar rant, we include a lesson designed to draw students' attention to some of grammar traps discussed in this section. Students will also learn how to educate themselves on some of the trickier aspects of negotiating "correctness" in different situations. And they'll have the opportunity to think critically about the attention paid to grammar in our society.

Critical thinking questions: Truss (2003) says famous writers can write comma splices, but Kalkavage (1998) says run-on sentences demonstrate "intellectual hiatus." Are famous writers just too dumb to follow the rules? Or, is this situation more complicated than it seems?

What's a Writer to Do? Become a Savvy Writer

When there are so many grammar traps out there for a writer to fall into, what can one do to avoid them? When students are held to higher standards than professional writers (who are allowed to break rules and who have professional copy editors to help them proofread), when readers read their writing looking for errors, when their readers almost always have more power than they do and can hold them hostage to their personal whims and pet peeves, how can students learn to be successful writers? Their teachers should help them become what we call savvy writers.

Savvy writers know that sometimes they can break commonly believed rules. Other times, however, appearing to break a rule that not even everyone considers a rule at all is a very bad idea. Savvy writers consider whom they are writing for and what those readers will think about them if they break the rule. If breaking a rule is a good risk, they break it. If it's a bad risk, they don't. Sometimes writing is like playing poker! Savvy writers also know that professional writing contexts often follow specific style guides or have their own style sheets. These writers do the research required to find those style guides so they can use them to make language choices. One of the best things teachers can do for their students is to select a classroom style and usage guide (or even better, negotiate a department or school style guide) and help the students learn to use it. Of course, students should not be taught that this is the only style guide available—that would be tantamount to telling them that football is the best sport or that cheddar cheese is the only good cheese. Selecting a style guide for students has at least two advantages that can help students become savvy writers:

1. It allows the students to see that language rules are not some abstract notion that only some people understand. They are concrete decisions that are made and agreed to by people who choose to follow a particular standard.

2. It allows students the ability to research and find useful answers to their language usage and style issues, so they aren't just being held to someone's personal preferences. Also, selecting a published standard for the class allows students to challenge a teacher if he or she is held to an improper standard regarding style or usage.

The marked-up grammar rant and lesson that follow offer opportunities for teachers and students to discuss the confusing state of some grammar

---

What savvy writers do: Savvy writers take risks in their writing, but if they are writing for a grade, they make sure their graders will accept experimentation. Sometimes students just ask their teachers outright if they will accept such writing as "deliberate fragments." But sometimes even *asking* such a question could be a risk.

What savvy writers do: In very important documents—job applications, college admissions essays, standardized exams, and so on—it's probably best to break as few rules of standardized English as possible. Unless you can be sure your readers will appreciate—or even tolerate—informed deviations from standardized English, it's probably better not to take the risk with documents that could have a dramatic effect on your future.

---

rules. Savvy writers know which rules are really traps and how to negotiate them as well as possible, so they can enter new writing territory equipped with the confidence and know-how to be successful.

Marked-Up Grammar Rant

"Good Grammar Gets Its Day"

by Andrew Dunn

The Daily Tar Heel (March 3, 2008)

When sophomore [Bill Jones*] is listening to a story, he won't hesitate to interrupt it in the name of grammar.

"If they say, 'Sally and me went to the movies,' I'll stop them and say, 'Sally and I.' It can be at the most crucial part of the story, but I will stop it and fix it," he said.

"Dude, I hate when people misuse grammar."

Today, magicians of the modifiers and geniuses of the gerunds can take heart, for it is National Grammar Day.

Sponsored by the Society for the Promotion of Good Grammar and the Microsoft Encarta encyclopedia, the day is intended to honor the English language and to emphasize the importance of proper syntax.

"If we don't respect and honor the rules of English, we lose our ability to communicate clearly and well," the day's official Web site states.

> If we take this seriously, this means Jones deliberately focuses on the surface aspects of any story he is listening to. First, this means he's not listening closely to the actual story. Second, he is certainly being quite disrespectful to the storyteller. How many people have stopped talking to him as a result of his rudeness?

> Dunn's use of alliteration here is clearly humorous—and it works.

> There are others for whom *dude* is a pet peeve. This may show a glint of humor, but it's hard to tell if he's being funny on purpose or if he's just making fun of other people. Given his attitude, it's probably the latter.

> The purpose of English is to communicate. We don't write and speak to "honor and respect" rules. We write and speak to communicate. We follow rules in order to communicate effectively, but we do not honor English. Why would someone want to honor a tool? Should we have National Hammer Day? Nut and Bolt Week?

> There is no such thing as *the* English language—one English language. There are actually many forms of English. There is an academic journal entitled *World Englishes*.

> "The rules of English" change over time, as they reflect the natural evolution of a language. These rules can have many exceptions, and different contexts can honor different conventions. Also, although something like "Sally and me went to the movies" is not standardized English, it is not unclear.

---

* Names of students in this article have been changed from the original.

Again the alliteration here signals a certain level of intended humor, but it's frequently the case that grammar ranters hyperbolize the effects of breaking grammar rules.

Gospel might be mentioned here because it begins with g, and the writer seems to love alliteration ("gospel of grammar"). But the religious overtone is not unusual in rants about grammar.

"In short, we invite mayhem, misery, madness and inevitably even more bad things that start with letters other than M."

How to celebrate? The grammar society recommends spreading of the gospel grammar.

"If you see a sign with a catastrophic apostrophe, send a kind note to the storekeeper," the Web site states. "If your local newscaster says, 'Between you and I,' set him straight with a friendly e-mail."

Also suggested are grammar potluck dinners, serving high-fiber foods. They're good for the colon.

But some students at UNC take their grammar a bit more seriously.

Sophomore [Jessica Brown] said she became dedicated to proper English during her junior year of high school.

Some readers consider the pun to be the lowest form of humor. (But we like puns.)

It would be an interesting, and difficult, rhetorical project: composing a "kind" note that is meant to correct a storekeeper's grammar.

Dedicated is another word with religious or righteous connotations.

Lie and lay are not the easiest verbs to conjugate. It's interesting that Brown is "particularly bothered" by errors involving these highly irregular verbs. It would make more sense to be "particularly bothered" when a writer makes a mistake with a regular verb that is easy to conjugate.

The idea of "spreading" good grammar, like Christianity, makes it seem like grammar ranters are on a mission to convert others from their evil ways.

She is particularly bothered by errors with "lie" and "lay" but enjoys parsing the differences between "who" and "whom."

One wonders who Brown's audience is for this parsing show.

Now, [Brown] said, she has trained herself to pay attention to grammatical errors in her friends' speech and corrects them when necessary.

"I don't say it to be superior or anything; I say it to help them," [Brown] said.

"At this age there is so much opportunity. We need to know how to speak intelligently."

She said she has converted her best friend and housemate, sophomore [Emma Burns], into a grammar aficionado.

"We talk about grammar all the time now," [Brown] said.

She added that grammar errors are not hard to fix, if people would just start learning basic grammar principles and noticing the errors in their speech.

"It's so effortless once you learn the fundamentals," she said. "It becomes a habit."

But UNC English professor Connie Elbe was not quite so extreme.

"I am not certain that formal training in grammar is necessary, or even important," Elbe wrote in an e-mail.

"I do think that the precise, clear and careful use of language is important. Insofar as the effective use of the language requires attention to grammatical structure, to that extent grammar is important."

Is it ever necessary to correct friends? Maybe if they are about to embarrass themselves, but that's probably it.

Here is the typical link: correct grammar = intelligent person. It's not true.

Converted also has religious connotations.

An *aficionado* is a fan or enthusiast. Being a grammar aficionado would mean being fascinated by how grammar works and shifts and changes in contexts and over time—an interest we share. From the context of this article, what Burns has become is a grammar "snob," one who insists that some grammars are inherently better than others and that those who disagree are wrong and must be corrected.

Brown says she's not correcting her friends "to be superior or anything." It would be interesting to interview her corrected friends and see how many of them feel helped. Assuming you know better than other people and offering them unsolicited correcting is a textbook example of "being superior." We suspect she is quite aware of her sense of superiority and that she's just showing false modesty to appease her guilt. Much about language use is actually quite personal and psychological.

Dunn characterizes Elbe's comment as "not quite so extreme," but it's actually the opposite of what Brown and others in the article claim. Elbe says she's not even sure that grammar instruction is even "necessary"!

"Basic grammar principles" would not be terribly helpful to speakers trying to conjugate *lie* and *lay*, which are irregular verbs. And knowing when to use *who* and *whom* is not all that "basic," either. These usages are not "fundamentals," nor do technical errors in them usually cause any confusion at all.

The Grammar Trap

Lesson 1

Objectives

Students will:

- note the level of emotional reaction by some readers/listeners to pronoun errors, especially those that do not interfere with meaning
- review rules, exceptions, and different conventions regarding nominative and objective pronouns
- explore language change
- think critically about the word choices, claims, and priorities of published writers who rant about these and other errors

Materials

- At least one grammar handbook for the class
- Internet access
- Handout 1: Warm-up (p. 113)
- Handout 2: Questions on "Good Grammar Gets Its Day" (p. 116)
- *Optional*: Access to *Garner's Modern American Usage* (Garner 2009)

Procedures

1. Warm-up exercise: Give students the warm-up handout and discuss it.

2. Have students read "Good Grammar Gets Its Day," by Andrew Dunn, which appeared in *The Daily Tar Heel* on March 3, 2008.

3. In large or small groups, have students discuss the questions on Handout 2.

Handout 1: WARM-UP

In mid-December, 2008, then President-elect Barack Obama nominated Arne Duncan to be the next Secretary of Education. In a statement following this nomination, Mr. Duncan said many things. However, the thirty-three-second video clip of his speech that dominated blog sites for days contained the following phrase, which grammar ranters gleefully foregrounded: "He gave my sister and I the opportunity to start a great school." The grammar ranters pointed out—usually in their very first sentence about Duncan's long speech—that Duncan should have said, "He gave my sister and *me*. . . ."

1. Why is this the kind of error that only people who are *attempting* to speak well make? What might be a logical reason Mr. Duncan said "He gave my sister and I" instead of "He gave my sister and me"?

2. Why are some people so eager to point out a grammar problem they see in Mr. Duncan's sentence?

3. Who do you think is more likely to pounce on Mr. Duncan's error, those who voted for Mr. Obama or those who did not vote for him? Why?

4. Why is Mr. Duncan an especially attractive target for criticism when he makes an error in grammar?

"Good Grammar Gets Its Day"

by Andrew Dunn

The Daily Tar Heel (March 3, 2008)

When sophomore [Bill Jones*] is listening to a story, he won't hesitate to interrupt it in the name of grammar.

"If they say, 'Sally and me went to the movies,' I'll stop them and say, 'Sally and I.' It can be at the most crucial part of the story, but I will stop it and fix it," he said.

"Dude, I hate when people misuse grammar."

Today, magicians of the modifiers and geniuses of the gerunds can take heart, for it is National Grammar Day.

Sponsored by the Society for the Promotion of Good Grammar and the Microsoft Encarta encyclopedia, the day is intended to honor the English language and to emphasize the importance of proper syntax.

"If we don't respect and honor the rules of English, we lose our ability to communicate clearly and well," the day's official Web site states.

"In short, we invite mayhem, misery, madness and inevitably even more bad things that start with letters other than M."

How to celebrate? The grammar society recommends spreading the gospel of grammar.

"If you see a sign with a catastrophic apostrophe, send a kind note to the storekeeper," the Web site states. "If your local newscaster says, 'Between you and I,' set him straight with a friendly e-mail."

Also suggested are grammar potluck dinners, serving high-fiber foods.

They're good for the colon.

But some students at UNC take their grammar a bit more seriously.

Sophomore [Jessica Brown] said she became dedicated to proper English during her junior year of high school.

She is particularly bothered by errors with "lie" and "lay" but enjoys parsing the differences between "who" and "whom."

Now, [Brown] said, she has trained herself to pay attention to grammatical errors in her friends' speech and corrects them when necessary.

---

* Students' names have been changed from the original.

"I don't say it to be superior or anything; I say it to help them," [Brown] said.

"At this age there is so much opportunity. We need to know how to speak intelligently."

She said she has converted her best friend and housemate, sophomore [Emma Burns], into a grammar aficionado.

"We talk about grammar all the time now," [Brown] said.

She added that grammar errors are not hard to fix, if people would just start learning basic grammar principles and noticing the errors in their speech.

"It's so effortless once you learn the fundamentals," she said. "It becomes a habit."

But UNC English professor Connie Elbe was not quite so extreme.

"I am not certain that formal training in grammar is necessary, or even important," Elbe wrote in an e-mail.

"I do think that the precise, clear and careful use of language is important. Insofar as the effective use of the language requires attention to grammatical structure, to that extent grammar is important."

Handout 2:
QUESTIONS ON "Good Grammar Gets Its Day"

1. If you were telling a story, would you want your friend to interrupt your story to correct your grammar? Why or why not?

2. What *is* the rule about the use of "Sally and me" or "Sally and I"? Look in a nearby grammar handbook or online grammar sites, such as the Purdue Online Writing Lab (http://owl.english.purdue.edu/) or "Grammar Girl Quick and Dirty Tricks" (http://grammar.quickanddirtytips.com/). Look under "nominative and objective pronouns."

3. Bill Jones, the sophomore who corrects people's use of pronouns, says this: "Dude, I hate when people misuse grammar." What might some adults think of his use of *dude*? How might Jones feel if someone interrupted *him* for his use of that word?

4. Google "National Grammar Day." Note how many newspapers and blogs covered this story. Why do you suppose there are so many hits on this event?

5. Visit the National Grammar Day website: http://nationalgrammarday.com/. (National Grammar Day was begun in 2008 by Martha Brockenbrough. The 2010 version was hosted by Mignon Fogerty, a/k/a Grammar Girl.) The March 4, 2010 celebration had a "Songwriting Hall of Shame," complete with a "cringe-worthy playlist" that included "Imma Be" by BEP, "Satisfaction" by the Rolling Stones, "Live and Let Die" by Paul McCartney and Wings, among others. Should song lyrics use formal grammar? Why or why not?

Answer Key for Handout 2

1. Answers will vary.

2. The explanations are too long to summarize here, but students visiting those sites will find what they need to know: In the United States, in formal English, as of this writing, *everybody* and *everyone* still take the singular form: "Everybody should bring his or her own towel." As Garner explains, however, Standard British English is different: "Today it is standard BrE to use *everyone* and *everybody* with a singular verb but a plural pronoun" (Garner 2009, 326).

3–5. Answers will vary.

Optional Writing Projects

- Rewrite some of the "incorrect" lyrics from the songs posted at the 2010 National Grammar Site ("Imma Be," "Satisfaction," etc.) so that they would satisfy the grammar mavens who object to the original lyrics. Are the songs better? What do the songs gain from the "correct" lyrics? Do they lose anything? Explain. Write a letter to the artists, taking issue with, or supporting, the language choices in their song lyrics.
- Write a letter or online comment to the folks at the National Grammar Day website, expressing your opinion on their "cringe-worthy playlist" of songs.

Further Research

- Are there any exceptions to the rules about when to use nominative or objective case pronouns? (See Garner 2009 or look in other editions of Bryan Garner's book under "pronouns.")
- Read what Garner says about "hypercorrection" (2009, 432) and the "Between you and me" issue (102–103). Who or what may be causing hypercorrectness?
- Go back to the National Grammar Day website. Also visit the website for "The Society for the Promotion of Good Grammar" (http://grammatically.blogspot.com/) as well as Grammar Girl website. How do they differ in tone? Which ones, if any, are helpful? Which ones, if any, are annoying?

- Google "'my sister and I' and Arne Duncan," and see how many hits you get. Follow the links on some of the news stories and blogs. Read some of the comments related to this incident. What is the tone? How much space do these writers take up on Duncan's pronoun choice (in proportion to the space they devote to education policy issues discussed in his speech)? What do you think of these stories and blogs? Why do people write them?
- How long does it take for a "mistake" to become part of accepted usage? Look up *often* in several new and old dictionaries and online. How is that word pronounced? How has its preferred pronunciation changed? Why do you think many people pronounce the *t* in *often*? Look up *disinterested* in a variety of old, new, and comprehensive dictionaries or usage manuals. What's the history of its meaning? Do the same with *inflammable*. Can you think of other words whose meaning has changed over time? What does this phenomenon tell you about language, people, and notions of correctness?
- Read Ken Lindblom's (2006) *English Journal* column, "Unintelligent Design: Where Does the Obsession with Correct Grammar Come From?" What do you think about his arguments regarding the use of *I* in the objective case as an example of understandable hyperformalism?
- Read "Dude," by Scott F. Kiesling (2004).

Further Activities

1. Many people use Strunk and White's *Elements of Style* (2005) as *the* authoritative handbook. Read "Happy Birthday, Strunk and White!" (2009), from *New York Times* blog, for the different views of the new edition of the famous *Elements of Style*. (Google "Happy Birthday Strunk and White!") See also an essay in *The Chronicle of Higher Education* written by Geoffrey K. Pullam, "Fifty Years of Stupid Grammar Advice" (2009).

2. In January, 2009, the City Council of Birmingham, England, ruled that apostrophes would no longer be used on road signs. This decision caused an uproar, and the Apostrophe Protection Society was not at all pleased.

   a. Google "apostrophes and Birmingham." How many hits did you find?
   b. Look at some of the verbs used in these brief news stories. What are some of the connotations of those verbs?

c. Do you think this is an important story? Why or why not? Why was this incident covered so heavily?

d. Who decides what is newsworthy? What stories in the world are not covered heavily, or covered at all? How do we find out about stories not covered by mainstream news outlets?

3. Visit the Apostrophe Protection Society online (www.apostrophe.org.uk/). At that site, it says, "Apostrophes are NEVER ever used to denote plurals!" Look up apostrophes and plurals in grammar handbooks or online. To what extent is that a correct statement? If possible, read Garner's entries on plurals of acronyms and abbreviations, and plurals of numbers and decades and words and letters (2009, 638–39). Or, use whatever edition is available, and look up those topics. FYI for instructors: *The Chicago Manual of Style* used to allow an apostrophe to make a plural in the case of words in quotation marks. So this sentence would have been correct: There were five "to be continued's" in the book series. However, the fifteenth edition changed that. This is a minor point, but it does show that the Apostrophe Protection Society site was incorrect when it issued its declaration.*

4. Become an authority on the serial comma. Google "serial comma" and see how many hits you get. Visit the Wikipedia entry on the serial comma. Look at the style sheets and handbooks supporting it or not supporting it. See what whatever grammar handbooks (paper or online) you have access to say about the serial comma. Which sentences need that last comma in order to prevent confusion? Which sentences would be clear and unambiguous with or without that final comma? Do the grammar handbooks you examine mention anything about how *context* plays a role in the rightness of the serial comma? Read your local or school newspaper. Look for sentences that tell you what that paper's style sheet must say about commas and words in a series. Look at *The New York Times, The Chicago Tribune,* or other newspapers available on the web. How do they handle it? How do your textbooks handle it? What about articles and advertisements in *Wired, Newsweek, Seventeen,* or other magazines? Try to get a copy of these publications' style sheets.

---

* We would like to thank Theresa Kay for informing us about this change in *The Chicago Manual of Style.*

5. Want help finding the latest grammar rants? Set a Google Alert for "grammar rants," "correct grammar," "proper grammar," among others. To set a Google Alert, go to the Google main site. Choose "Language Tools," then "More," then "Even more." Then click on "Alerts" and follow the directions. It's easy.

Further Writing Projects on Grammar Traps

- Is this attention to comma splices much ado about nothing? Imagine that in a later edition of this book, *Grammar Rants*, you are invited to write an Afterword in which you get to comment on this book and the whole issue of comma splices, fragments, and the rest. What might you say in 250–500 words?
- Have any of your sentences ever been pointed out as comma splices, run-ons, or fragments? Do you agree that they were, in fact, comma splices, or run-ons, or fragments? Were any of them arguably "justifiable comma splices" or "stylistic fragments"? If your sentences were actually wrong, would you know how to fix them now? If you think they were "justifiable comma splices" or "stylistic fragments," what are some pros and cons to making this argument to your reader? Can student writers ever practice poetic license? Write a letter to your instructor (or to the English Department) arguing for or against the idea of students using justifiable comma splices or stylistic fragments.
- Complete Activity 4 (p. 119). Once you've become an authority on the "serial comma," imagine that your class or school has its own style sheet, written collaboratively by teachers and students. Suppose it's your task to write the entry on the serial comma and how to handle words or phrases in a series. How would you explain "the rules" clearly and concisely? What examples would you use?

Further Readings

For a comprehensive history of the apostrophe, read Elizabeth S. Sklar's article, "The Possessive Apostrophe: The Development and Decline of a Crooked Mark" in *College English* (October 1976, 175–83).

For an informative and humorous look at the English language, read Bill Bryson's chapter, "Good English and Bad," from *Mother Tongue: English and How It Got That Way* (1990, 134–46).

For an insightful examination of usage in English Language, see Edgar H. Schuster's "Chapter 3: Usage: Rules That Do Not Rule (and a Few That Do)" in *Breaking the Rules: Liberating Writers Through Innovative Grammar Instruction* (Schuster 2003).

For an interesting take on how grammar handbooks handle the pronoun controversy, see Sharon Zubar and Anne M. Reed's article, "The Politics of Grammar Handbooks: Generic He and Singular They" in *College English* (September 1993, 515–30).

For a comprehensive and well-written discussion of grammar controversies, read David Foster Wallace's essay in *Harper's Magazine*: "Tense Present: Democracy, English, and the Wars over Usage" (April 2001; available at www.harpers.org/media/pdf/dfw/HarpersMagazine-2001-04-0070913.pdf).

For comprehensive background on "error," plus some surprises, read *Garner's Modern American Usage* (Third Edition) entries on "Superstitions" (Garner 2009, 786–88).

For a history of punctuation, read "Comma Before the Storm," by Judith Stone in *Discover* (July 1990, 32–35).

For an account of how one person can affect language change, or lack thereof, read "Language, Commas, and the Unmistakable Sound, of 'The New Yorker,'" by Ben Yagoda, in *The Chronicle of Higher Education* (October 17, 1997; Opinion, B9+). In fact, Ben Yagoda's website (www.benyagoda.com/) is a treasure trove of books and articles on language use.

For more information and for earlier versions of some of the arguments we make in this book, see our articles and essays:

Lindblom, Kenneth, and Patricia A. Dunn. 2006. "Analyzing Grammar Rants: An Alternative to Traditional Grammar Instruction." *English Journal* 95.5 (May): 71–77.

Dunn, Patricia A., and Kenneth J. Lindblom. 2003. "Why Revitalize Grammar?" *English Journal* 92.3 (January): 43–50.

Dunn, Patricia A., and Kenneth Lindblom. 2005. "Developing Savvy Writers by Analyzing Grammar Rants." In *Language in the School Curriculum: Integrating Linguistic Knowledge into K–12 Teaching*, edited by Kristin Denham and Anne Lobeck, 191–207. Mahwah, NJ: Lawrence Erlbaum Associates.

Works Cited

Aaron, Jane E. 2007. *The Little, Brown Compact Handbook.* 6th ed. New York: Pearson/Longman.

Adams, Stephen. 2009. "Apostrophe Now: Backlash Begins." www.telegraph. co.uk/news/uknews/4401474/Apostrophe-now-backlash-begins.html (January 31).

Associated Press. 2004. "National Spelling Bee kicks off in D.C." *The Anchorage Daily News* (June 1). Available at www.adn.com/24hour/nation/v-printer/ story/1407610p-8699641c.html.

———. 2007. "Phony Fax Gives Prisoner Almost 2 Weeks of Freedom." (April 21). Available at www.thehelper.net/forums/showthread.php/ 56379-Phony-fax-gives-prisoner-almost-2-weeks-of-freedom?s= 6fe9da79b195abc397224730ec7e7f8c.

Associated Press (London). 2009. "It's a Catastrophe for the Apostrophe in Britain." (January 21).

Bergan, Dan. 2004. "Gramme(a)r: Using It and It's." *The Daily Tribune* (March 18).

Bonilla, Denise M. 2004. "This 'Rober' Means 'Bizness.'" (January 24). Available at www.policeone.com/news/79051-police-seek-spelling-bee-dropout-linked- to-7-bank-holdups.

Bremner, John B. 1980. *Words on Words: A Dictionary for Writers and Others Who Care About Words.* New York: Columbia University Press.

British Academy. 2010. "LITER8 LRNRS: IS TEXTING VALUABLE OR VANDALISM?" Available at www.britac.ac.uk/news/news.cfm/newsid/14.

Britton, James. 1994. "Shaping at the Point of Utterance." Reprinted in *Landmark Essays on Invention in Writing,* edited by Richard E. Young and Yameng Liu, 147–52. Anaheim, CA: Hermagoras Press.

Bryson, Bill. 1990. "Good English and Bad." In *Mother Tongue: English and How It Got That Way,* 134–46. New York: HarperCollins.

Casagrande, June. 2009. "A Word Please." www.kilgorenewsherald.com/news/2009-01-04/lifestyles/034.html. January 4.

"Case of the Serial Comma." 2005. Professional Training Company: Communications Strategies for Scientists and Engineers. (November 23). Available at www.protrainco.com/essays/serial-comma.htm.

The Chicago Manual of Style: The Essential Guide for Writers, Editors, and Publishers, 15 ed. 2003. Chicago: University of Chicago Press.

Chivers, Tom. 2009. "Internet Rules and Laws: The Top 10, from Godwin to Poe." *The Telegraph.* October 23. www.telegraph.co.uk/technology/news/6408927/Internet-rules-and-laws-the-top-10-from-Godwin-to-Poe.html.

Christian, Darrell, Sally Jacobsen, and David Minthorn. Eds. 2009. *The Associated Press Style Book and Briefing on Media Law.* New York: Basic Books.

Clio, Max. 2003. "Grading on My Nerves." *The Chronicle of Higher Education* 50 (13): C2. Available at http://chronicle.com/jobs/news/2003/11/2003111801c.htm.

Coughlan, Sean. 2010. "Phone Texting 'Helps Pupils to Spell.'" Available at http://news.bbc.co.uk/2/hi/uk_news/education/8468351.stm.

Crowley, Sharon, and Debra Hawhee. 2009. *Ancient Rhetorics for Contemporary Students,* 4th ed. New York: Pearson.

Cullen, Richard. 2008. "Did the New EdSec Just Make a Grammatical Error?" Politico.com. www.politico.com/blogs/anneschroeder/1208/Did_the_new_EdSec_just_make_a_grammatical_error_.html.

Deck, Jeff, and Benjamin D. Herson. 2010. *The Great Typo Hunt: Two Friends Changing the World One Correction at a Time.* New York: Crown.

Dickinson, Emily. 1961. *Final Harvest: Emily Dickinson's Poems.* Boston: Little, Brown.

Dunn, Andrew. 2008. "Good Grammar Gets Its Day." *The Daily Tar Heel* (March 3).

Dunn, Patricia A. 2001. *Talking, Sketching, Moving: Multiple Literacies and the Teaching of Writing.* Portsmouth, NH: Boynton/Cook.

Dunn, Patricia A., and Kenneth J. Lindblom. 2003. "Why Revitalize Grammar?" *English Journal* 92 (3): 43–50.

———. 2005. "Developing Savvy Writers by Analyzing Grammar Rants." In *Language in the School Curriculum: Integrating Linguistic Knowledge into K–12 Teaching,* edited by Kristin Denham and Anne Lobeck, 191–207. Mahwah, NJ: Lawrence Erlbaum Associates.

Felmley, David. 1915. "Bridgewater and the Normal Schools of the West." In *Seventy-Fifth Anniversary of the State Normal School, Bridgewater, Massachusetts, June 19, 1915,* 19–24. Bridgewater, MA: A. H. Willis.

Gage, Joan Paulson. 2010. "Michelle Obama, the Grammar Police & a Cranky Crone." A Rolling Crone. (April 14). Available at http://arollingcrone. blogspot.com/2010/04/michelle-obama-grammar-police-cranky.html.

Garner, Bryan A. 2009. *Garner's Modern American Usage.* 3d ed. Oxford, UK: Oxford University Press.

Garrett, Kristen. 2005. "Grammar Gaffes." *Times Online (Beaver County Times & Allegheny Times)* (November 25).

Gee, James. 2007. *What Video Games Have to Teach Us About Learning and Literacy,* 2d ed., revised and updated. New York: Palgrave Macmillan.

Gibaldi, Joseph, ed. 1999. *MLA Handbook for Writers of Research Papers,* 5th ed. New York: The Modern Language Association of America.

Graham, Steve, and Delores Perin. 2007. "A Meta-Analysis of Writing Instruction for Adolescent Students." *Journal of Educational Psychology* 99 (3): 445–76.

Hale, Constance. 1999. *Sin and Syntax.* New York: Broadway Books.

"Happy Birthday, Strunk and White!" 2009. Opinion. *The New York Times.* Available at http://roomfordebate.blogs.nytimes.com/2009/04/24/happy-birthday-strunk-and-white/.

Harmon, Sandra D. 1995. "'The Voice, Pen and Influence of Our Women Are Abroad in the Land': Women and the Illinois State Normal University, 1857–1899." In *Nineteenth-Century Women Learn to Write,* edited by Catherine Hobbs, 84–102. Charlottesville: University Press of Virginia.

Harper, Charles A. 1935. *Development of the Teachers College in the United States with Special Reference to the Illinois State Normal University.* Bloomington, IN: McKnight and McKnight.

Heyl, Eric. 2003. "It's a Crime Grammar Means Little to Robber." *Pittsburgh Tribune-Review* (January 18): 1–2. Available at www.pittsburghlive.com/x/pittsburghtrib/s_113477.html.

Hubert, Cynthia. 2008. "Teens' Texting Symbols Invade Schoolwork :-(." *The Sacramento Bee* (April 25). Available at www.sacbee.com/101/v-print/story/889102.htm. Accessed April 25, 2008.

Hunt, Bud, and Tiffany J. Hunt, eds. 2006. "Whose Grammar for What Purposes?" *English Journal* 95 (5): 88–92.

Ijams, Chrissy. 2004. "Correcting Great Wrongs Has Been a Lifelong Obsession." *The Modesto Bee* (March 1). Available at www.modbee.com/opinion/community/story/8214735p-9064455c.html. Retrieved March 2004.

"It's Time to Rest a Spell." 2002. Editorial. *The Pantagraph* (June 1): A14.

Johnson, Steven. 2005. *Everything Bad Is Good for You*. New York: Penguin.

Johnson, Walter H. 2006. "The Sentence-Structure Dilemma." *English Journal* 95 (3): 14–15.

Kalkavage, Peter. 1998. "Student Writing and the Trouble with Grammar." *Education Digest* 63 (7): 58–61.

Kiester, Jane Bell. 1998, 2003. *The Chortling Bard: Caught-ya! Grammar with a Giggle for High School*. Gainesville, FL: Maupin House.

Kiesling, Scott F. 2004. "Dude." *American Speech* 79 (3): 221–305.

Lears, Jackson. 2003. *Something for Nothing: Luck in America*. New York: Penguin.

Lenhart, Amanda, Sousan Arafeh, Aaron Smith, and Alexandra Macgill. 2008. "Writing, Technology & Teens: Findings of the Pew Internet & American Life Project and the National Commission on Writing." (April 24). www.pewtrusts.org/uploadedFiles/wwwpewtrustsorg/Reports/Society_and_the_Internet/PIP_Writing_Report_FINAL.pdf.

Lewin, Tamar. 2008. "Informal Style of Electronic Messages Is Showing Up in Schoolwork, Study Finds" *The New York Times* (April 25). Available at www.nytimes.com/2008/04/25/education/25writing.html. Accessed April 28, 2008.

Lindblom, Kenneth. 2006. "Unintelligent Design: Where Does the Obsession with Correct Grammar Come From?" *English Journal* 95 (5): 93–97.

Lindblom, Kenneth, and Patricia A. Dunn. 2006. "Analyzing Grammar Rants: An Alternative to Traditional Grammar Instruction." *English Journal* 95 (5): 71–77.

Lindblom, Kenneth, Will Banks, and Rise Quay. 2007. "Mid-Nineteenth-Century Writing Instruction at Illinois State Normal University: Credentials, Correctness and the Rise of a Teaching Class." In *Local Histories: Reading the Archives of Composition*, edited by Patricia Donahue and Gretchen Flesher Moon, 94–114. Pittsburgh: University of Pittsburgh Press.

Loda, Rebecca. 2002. "Lincoln Speller's Run Ends in Round 3." *The Pantagraph* (May 31): A1.

Long, Judith. 2004. "Lynne Truss High Priestess of Punctuation: Comma Sutra." Newsday.com. May 9. www.newsday.com/features/booksmags/ny—bktalk0509.0.403038041.story?coll=ny-bookreview-headlines.

Lynn, David H. 1993. "Are Grammarians Antiquarians in an Information Age?" *Education Digest* 59 (2): 68–69.

Maslin, Janet. 2004. "Hark, Abused Punctuation: This Writer Feels Your Pain." Books of the Times. *The New York Times* (April 8). Available at http://query.nytimes.com/gst/fullpage.html?res= 9400EED71738F93BA35757C0A9629C8B63.

Mayher, John S. 1990. *Uncommon Sense: Theoretical Practice in Language Education.* Portsmouth, NH: Boynton/Cook.

McCourt, Frank. 2004. Foreword to *Eats, Shoots & Leaves: The Zero Tolerance Approach to Punctuation,* by Lynne Truss. New York: Gotham Books.

Mills, Richard. 2004. "A Retrospective on Reform and High Standards." *Long Island Education Review* 4 (2): 10–11.

Molyneux, Ann. 2006. "Duz it Relly Mater if We Cant Spel Properly?" *Peterborough Today* (November 22). Available at www.peterboroughtoday.co.uk/ news/environment/duz_it_relly_mater_if_we_cant_spel_properly_1_69425.

Nelson, Jim. 2004. "Baseball and Correct Grammar Don't Always Mix." *Bluefield Daily Telegraph* (May 12). Available at at www.author-me.com/nonfiction/ baseballandgrammar.htm.

Noguchi, Rei R. 1991. *Grammar and the Teaching of Writing: Limits and Possibilities.* Urbana, IL: National Council of Teachers of English.

O'Reilly, Bill. 2003. "'People's Choice' Eminem Demeans Our Basic Values." *The Pantagraph* (January 19): C4.

Pareen, Alex. 2008. "Our Stupid New Education Secretary Said Something Stupid!" December 16. http://gawker.com/5111715/our-stupid-new-education-secretary-said-something-stupid.

Phillips, P., and J. Phillips. 2002. "Dear Abby: Good Grammar Magic to Her Ears." *The Pantagraph* (April 9): D2.

"The Pitfalls of Text-Messaging." 2007. *The Western Courier* (April 27). Available at http://media.www.westerncourier.com/media/storage/paper650/news/ 2007/04/27/Opinion/The-Pitfalls.Of.TextMessaging-2886139.shtml.

Plester, Beverly, and Clare Wood. 2009. "Exploring Relationships Between Traditional and New Media Literacies: British Preteen Texters at School." *Journal of Computer-Mediated Communication* 14: 1108–29.

Proulx, Annie. 1999. "The Blood Bay." In *Close Range: Wyoming Stories.* New York: Scribner.

———. 2004. "Man Crawling Out of Trees." In *Bad Dirt: Wyoming Stories 2.* New York: Scribner.

Pullam, Geoffrey K. 2009. "Fifty Years of Stupid Grammar Advice" Available at http://chronicle.com/article/50-Years-of-Stupid-Grammar/25497.

Rabinovitch, Simon. 2007. "Thousands of Hyphens Perish as English Marches On." Reuters. (September 21). Available at www.reuters.com/article/idUSHAR15384620070921.

Rosenstock, Bonnie. 2005. "The Great St. Mark/Mark's Punctuation Debate Solved." *The Villager* 74 (55). Available at www.thevillager.com/villager_108/thegreatstmarksmarks.html.

Schemo, Diana Jean. 2004. "In Online Auctions, Misspelling in Ads Often Spells Cash." *The New York Times* (January 28). Available at www.nytimes.com/2004/01/28/technology/28SPEL.html.

Schneider, Howard. 2010. Center for News Literacy. Available at www.stonybrook.edu/journalism/newsliteracy/index.html. Retrieved July 1.

Schuster, Edgar. 2003. *Breaking the Rules: Liberating Writers Through Innovative Writing Instruction*. Portsmouth, NH: Heinemann.

———. 2006. "A Fresh Look at Sentence Fragments." *English Journal* 95 (5): 78–83.

Scott, Sonny. 2006. "Clear Thinking Resides in Correct Grammar." *Northeast Mississippi Daily Journal* (October 29).

Simmons, Tracy Lee. 2000. "Getting the Words Right: How to Teach—and Not Teach—Writing." *National Review* 52 (17): 48–49.

Sklar, Elizabeth S. 1976. "The Possessive Apostrophe: The Development and Decline of a Crooked Mark." *College English* 38 (2): 175–83.

Smithstein, Samantha. 2010. "Too Easy to Say 'I h8 u' (and More Potential Pitfalls of Texting for Teens)." *Psychology Today* (May 4). Available at www.psychologytoday.com/print/42069.

"Spelling Bee Claims at Least One from Area." 2010. Staff report. *Times Union* (June 4): D1, D7.

Stetson, Albert. 1867. "Spelling." In *Report of the Illinois Teachers' Institute Held at the Normal University, August 1867*, 110–13. Nason, IL: Illinois Teacher Office, Peoria.

Stone, Judith. 1990. "Comma Before the Storm." *Discover* (July): 32–35.

Strumpf, Michael, and Auriel Douglas. 1999. *The Grammar Bible*. New York: Henry Holt.

Strunk, William Jr., and E. B. White. 2005. *The Elements of Style*. Illustrated by Maira Kalman. New York: Penguin.

Thomas, Cal. 2000. "Coming Home to School." *Jewish World Review* (June 7). Available at www.jewishworldreview.com/cols/thomas060700.asp.

Truss, Lynne. 2003. *Eats, Shoots & Leaves: The Zero Tolerance Approach to Punctuation*. New York: Gotham Books.

Turner, Kristen Hawley. 2009. "Flipping the Switch: Code-Switching from Text Speak to Standard English." *English Journal* 98 (May): 60–65.

United States Census. Available at www.census.gov/compendia/statab/2010/tables/10s0228.pdf.

Vargas, Theresa. 2005. "Police: Misspellings Were Just a Ploy." *Newsday* (February 12). Available at www.newsday.com/news/local/longisland/ny-lispe10212.0.5318945.story?coll=ny-linews-headlines. Accessed February 13, 2005.

Walker, Jamesetta. 2006. "Apostrophe 's': We'll Add It to Everything." *Clarion Ledger* (February 26). Available at www.clarion.edger.com/apps/pbcs.dll/article?AID=/20060226/COL0206/602260315. Retrieved February 27, 2006.

Wallace, David Foster. 2001. "Tense Present: Democracy, English, and the Wars over Usage." *Harper's Magazine* April. Available at www.harpers.org/media/pdf/dfw/HarpersMagazine-2001-04-0070913.pdf.

Weiner, Randi. 2005. "Schools in N.Y. Give Grammar Short Shrift." *The Journal News* (October 24). Available at www.lohud.com/apps/pbcs.dll/article?AID=/20051024/NEWS03/510240317/1024/NEWS08&template=printart. Retrieved January 3, 2011.

White, Joseph. 2007. "California Teen Wins Bee with 'Serrefine.'" *The Villages Daily Sun* (June 1): A1, A6.

Williams, Joseph. 1981. "The Phenomenology of Error." *College Composition and Communication* 32 (2): 152–68.

Wykoff, George S., and Harry Shaw, eds. 1952. *The Harper Handbook of College Composition*, 3d ed. New York: Harper & Row.

Yagoda, Ben. 1997. "Language, Commas, and the Unmistakable Sound, of 'The New Yorker.'" *The Chronicle of Higher Education* (October 17): Opinion, B9+.

Zubar, Sharon, and Anne M. Reed. 1993. "The Politics of Grammar Handbooks: Generic He and Singular They." *College English* 55: 515–30.

Index

"Dear Abby," 32
Deck, Jeff, 26
details, lessons on, 71–74, 90–93
Dickinson, Emily, 2
"Dude," 118
Duncan, Arne, 97–98, 118
Dunn, Andrew, 109, 114
Dunn, Patricia, 34

Eats, Shoots & Leaves, 6, 27, 107
education, grammar rants about, 32–36
    lesson on, 44, 47–49
Edwards, Richard, 3, 52
Elements of Style, The, 99, 100, 107
Eminem, 5
Everybody Loves Raymond, 2
evil, bad grammar associated with, 1–4,
    6, 7, 76, 81, 110

"Fifty Years of Stupid Grammar
    Advice," 118
"Flipping the Switch: Code-Switching
    from Text Speak to Standard
    English," 77
Fogerty, Mignon, 116
fragments, 71, 102–107
    lesson on, 66
"A Fresh Look at Sentence Fragments,"
    71
fused sentence, 102, 103, 104

Gage, Joan, 97
Garner, Bryan, 93, 98
Garner's Modern American Usage, 42, 93,
    98, 121
Garrett, Kristen, 4–5
genres, lesson on, 83–90
gluttony, 8, 11, 19, 23,
"Good Grammar Gets Its Day," 109–11,
    114–16
The Grammar Bible, 4
Grammar Girl, 66, 69, 116, 117
grammar ranters, ix–x
    call for clarity of, 31–32
    targets of, 26, 29

grammar rants
    analyzing, xi–xii, 96
    assumptions of, 26
    connotations in, 17
    defined, x
    about education, 32–36
    inferences in, 18–19
    about intelligence, 26–32
    lessons on, 13–23, 40–49, 66–74
    moral rhetoric in, ix, 1–10
    problems caused by, x–xi, xiii–xiv
    shared assumptions of, 25–26
    and spelling, 50–65
    and standards, xiii
    about texting, 76–80
grammar traps, 94–95
    apostrophes, 101–102
    audience issues, 95
    avoiding, 108
    comma splices, 107
    possessive pronouns, 94–95
    pronoun case, 97–98
    serial comma, 99–101
Grammar and the Teaching of Writing,
    32
"Gramme(a)r: Using *Its* and *It's*,"
    11–13
The Great Typo Hunt, 26
greengrocers' apostrophe, 6

Harvard comma, 99
Herson, Benjamin, 26
Heyl, Eric, 59–61, 63–65, 67–68
Hubert, Cynthia, 76–78
Hunt, Bud and Tiffany, 99–100
hypercorrection, 33, 98, 117
hyphen loss, 80, 92

Ijams, Chrissy, 52
Illinois State Normal University, 2–3,
    51–52
implications, 17
    lesson on, 14–16, 18
independent clauses, comma splicing
    of, 107

Schneider, Howard, 80

Schuster, Edgar, xi, 2, 71, 121

Scott, Sonny, 31

Scripps National Spelling Bee, 55, 57
  lesson using, 71–74

serial comma, 99–101, 119

Simmons, Tracy Lee, 29–30, 31

Simplified Spelling Society, 52

Sin and Syntax, 4

Skapinker, Michael, 7

Sklar, Elizabeth S., 120

sloth, 2, 5, 19

Smithstein, Samantha, 78, 90

Something for Nothing, 8

spell-checkers, 51

spelling, 50
  equated with intelligence or
      knowledge, 57–58
  equated with moral failure, 58–62
  obsession with, 51–52
  in perspective, 53
  standardization of, 51

spelling bees, 51
  lessons about, 71–74
  news stories about, 54–58
  as sport, 54

Spelling Society, 52

standardized English, 9, 39, 80, 98, 108,
      109

standards, xiii

Stetson, Albert, 3

Stone, Judith, 121

Strunk and White. *See The Elements of Style*

Take the Money and Run, 61

Talking, Sketching, Moving, 34

Taylor, Greg, 62

"Teens Texting Symbols Invade
      Schoolwork :-(," 76, 85

"Tense Present," 121

texting, 4–5, 75–76
  effects on formal speech, 76–78
  prejudices about, 78–79

Thomas, Cal, 57

"Thousands of Hyphens Perish as
      English Marches On," 80

Truss, Lynn, 6, 27–28, 107

Turabian, Kate, 100

Turner, Kristen Hawley, 77

*The 25th Annual Putnam County Spelling
      Bee*, 55

"Unintelligent Design," 33, 51

voice-to-text, 51

Walker, Jamesetta, 5

Wallace, David Foster, 121

*Webster's Third New International
      Dictionary*, 57

Weiner, Randi, 26, 27, 28, 36–39, 41

Whole Language movement, 30

Williams, Joseph, xi

Wood, Clare, 90

word choice, 17
  lesson on, 14–16, 18

"Writing, Technology, and Teens," 75,
      77, 87–88

Young, Michael, 35, 97

Zubar, Sharon, 121